For the CUSPE

with best regards,

Liam Van Workhel

2 | 12 | 2020

St Antony's Series

Series Editors
Dan Healey
St Antony's College
University of Oxford
Oxford, UK

Leigh Payne
St Antony's College
University of Oxford
Oxford, UK

The St Antony's Series publishes studies of international affairs of contemporary interest to the scholarly community and a general yet informed readership. Contributors share a connection with St Antony's College, a world-renowned centre at the University of Oxford for research and teaching on global and regional issues. The series covers all parts of the world through both single-author monographs and edited volumes, and its titles come from a range of disciplines, including political science, history, and sociology. Over more than forty years, this partnership between St Antony's College and Palgrave Macmillan has produced about 300 publications.

More information about this series at
http://www.palgrave.com/gp/series/15036

Lieve Van Woensel

A Bias Radar for Responsible Policy-Making

Foresight-Based Scientific Advice

Lieve Van Woensel
Scientific Foresight Unit
European Parliamentary
Research Service
Brussels, Belgium

St Antony's Series
ISBN 978-3-030-32125-3   ISBN 978-3-030-32126-0   (eBook)
https://doi.org/10.1007/978-3-030-32126-0

Cover credit: Hufton+Crow-VIEW/Alamy Stock Photo

Disclaimer: The content of this book is the sole responsibility of the author and any
opinions expressed therein do not necessarily represent the official position of the European
Parliament for which the author works.

This Palgrave Pivot imprint is published by the registered company Springer Nature
Switzerland AG
The registered company address is: Gewerbestrasse 11, 6330 Cham, Switzerland

FOREWORD

I welcome this book, which is a guide to the use of scientific advice to inform policy and society, and to advise policy-makers on ways to approach science- and technology-related problems.

Ideally, policy-making should be evidence-based. However, democratic decision-making requires a careful balance between scientific evidence and other inputs, such as citizens' voices. This book addresses the issue of how the generation of scientific advice requires advisers to take a holistic approach and also looks at the need for advisers to check possible impacts of scientific and technical developments, including unintended ones.

Everyone in the science-policy ecosystem, as well as the citizen, is subject to biases. Biases can systematically distort our perceptions of facts and opinions and how advisers weigh evidence and make assessments. Dr Van Woensel describes a series of biases, which she presents in the form of a bias wheel. This provides a practical tool for everyone involved in policy-making to check their own and others' thinking for possible biases. She argues that bias awareness helps us to be more open-minded and more reflective when dealing with scientific evidence, especially when there can be emotion-based opinions when working on controversial issues, for example, with genetic engineering, nuclear technologies, chemical use and climate change.

With her experience working on scientific foresight for the European Parliament, she shares good practice on how to investigate topics from a wide range of perspectives. She also offers a guiding scheme that could help safeguard against possible consequences of new technologies being overlooked.

Lastly, she emphasizes that for each alternative direction that is possible for policy-makers based on the evidence provided by advisers, they need to investigate and describe possible impacts (positive and negative) on society. This is supplemented by providing simple practical steps to take to prevent overlooking adverse effects of implementing policies.

This book gives us a thoughtful consideration of how best to approach policy-making using a range of different types of evidence. Dr Van Woensel's suggested methodology helps us to address the perspectives of citizens, scientists and policy-makers and could help to increase the confidence they have in both the scientific evidence and the impact of new technologies. If we get this right, then we might be justified in thinking that confidence in policy-making might grow and that all citizens would see the benefit of the knowledge generated by science, engineering and technology. That is a worthy goal.

Professor Dame Anne Glover
Former Chief Scientific Adviser
to the President of the European
Commission

ACKNOWLEDGEMENTS

Though a lot of people have shaped this manuscript in direct and indirect ways, I would like to acknowledge some of them in particular.

First of all, I was extremely fortunate to have received the Senior EU Fellowship for 2017–2018 at the Centre for European Studies, St Antony's College, University of Oxford, where I was able to step out of the policy-advising bubble and dedicate time to the academic study of scientific advising and policy while attending inspiring seminars and meeting interesting academics. I express my thanks to Anthony Teasdale, Director-General of the European Parliamentary Research Services at the European Parliament, and Lowri Evans, Chair of the European Fellowship Committee, without whose encouragement this adventure would have never materialized.

I would like to acknowledge the contributions of all of my interviewees, who inspired me through their reflections on scientific evidence, policy and bias: Renuka Bahde, Rob Bellamy, Didier Bourguignon, Hans Bruyninckx, Kerstin Cuhls, Hubert Deluyker, Mady Delvaux, Robert Doubleday, Pearl Dykstra, Alexandra Freeman, Julie Girling, Dame Anne Glover, Sir Charles Godfray, Sharaelle Grzesiak, Wolfgang Hiller, James Hynard, Ana Jakil-Holzer, Eva Kaili, Theo Karapiperis, Johannes Klumpers, Christian Kurrer, Charlotte Medland, Riel Miller, Fientje Moerman, Jan Marco Muller, Nissy Nevil, Eamonn Noonan, Lesley Paterson, Kris Peeters II, Jerry Ravetz, Riccardo Ribera d'Alcala, Margarida Rodrigues, Paul Rübig, Maurizio Salvi, Raf Scheers, Keith Sequeira, Sir David Spiegelhalter, Karen Stroobants, Vladimir Sucha,

William Sutherland, Jaana Tapanainen, Anthony Teasdale, Chris Tyler, Sybille van den Hove, Kristel Van der Elst, Pieter Vandooren, Sofie Vanthournout, Koen Vermeir, Arūnas Vinčiūnas, Tracey Wait and Koen Wauters.

Many of the ideas in this book were developed in the course of lively exchanges with numerous colleagues at the European Parliament, especially Eamonn Noonan, Gianluca Quaglio, Philip Boucher, Suzana Anghel, Mihalis Kritikos, Christian Kurrer, Nera Kuljanic, Eszter Fay and Svetla Tanova. My particular gratitude goes to our trainees at the European Parliament: Darja Vrscaj, who helped shape our foresight practices in 2015; Vicky Joseph; Jens Van Steerteghem; Richelle Boone and Sophie Millar.

I am very grateful to the members of the Panel for the Future of Science and Technology (STOA) at the European Parliament for their support and contributions to the scientific advice toolkit, particularly Paul Rübig, a passionate supporter of this new approach to investigating the future of science and technology, and Mady Delvaux, my first professional foresight client with whom I had many inspiring conversations. I thank Julie Girling, Member of the European Parliament, who honoured me by being a discussant in my closing seminar at Oxford, where she became familiar with the concept of cognitive dissonance.

My colleagues and fellow fellows at Oxford's Centre for European Studies deserve my thanks, especially Yukari Akeda, for our conversations on bias; Cristina Blanco, who was always optimistic about my work; Hartmut Mayer, Director of the Centre for European Studies, who warmly welcomed me at the Centre; Kalypso Nicolaidis, who sponsored my fellowship; the other most inspiring professors and lecturers at the European Studies Centre, namely, Timothy Garton Ash, Paul Betts, Jan Zielonka and Othon Anastasakis, who are all prominent experts in their disciplines, and Lucas Kello, Director of the Centre for Technology and Global Affairs at Oxford, who studies technology from the perspective of international relations. They made me understand that people from different disciplines reason in different ways that enrich each other. Many debates held at the Oxford Martin School contributed to the ideas developed in this book, such as the doughnut scheme for assessing policy, which I developed after a talk with Kate Raworth. Special thanks go to Rafael Ramirez, Director of the Oxford Scenarios Program, for his stimulating reflections and for introducing me to various experts with distinct views and backgrounds. Finally, I cherished my talks with Jerry Ravetz, the developer and an active ambassador of 'post-normal science'.

My heartfelt gratitude goes to Kristel Van der Elst, a bright futurist who introduced me to foresight and scenario thinking and encouraged me through her interest in my work, and to Tsjalling Swierstra for sharing his understanding of the soft impacts of technology. I thank Dame Anne Glover for sharing her inspiring views in thought-provoking dialogues and her encouragement, Theo Compernolle for his interest in my research and for an illuminating exchange on reflective and reflexive thinking in policy-making and Bruno Hoste for our conversations about the human mind. I also thank Arne van Stiphout for his enthusiastic technical input on electric cars.

I am grateful to Theo Karapiperis, who has long worked in technology assessment, for his conscientious reading of the manuscript and his constructive suggestions to improve it.

I thank the colleagues, friends and family whose questions considerably sharpened the ideas in this book.

My heartfelt thanks go to everyone else who has helped me along the way, with apologies to those I have inadvertently not mentioned.

While any errors, twisted thinking or unclear expressions in this book are my sole responsibility, Greg Sax, my critical editor, challenged me to clearly and logically formulate my ideas. His contributions have been essential to improving the logic and clarity of this book.

I warmly thank my brother Peter for his artistic input to envisioning a world with rising sea levels.

Last to be acknowledged, but first in all other respects, is my husband Hendrik, whose support of my Oxford adventure; patience while I was writing and keen interest and many challenging thoughts on scientific facts, perception, citizenship and policy have inspired me in every step.

And, finally, while writing this book I had the pleasure of being faithfully accompanied by our beautiful black and white, purring cat.

INTRODUCTION

This book is about responsible scientific advisory practices in the context of policy-making. It is obvious that policy should be based on scientific evidence. However, this book goes beyond that claim and focuses on policy advice beyond that evidence.

I focus on how policy advisers deal with evidence in general and specifically on how they assess it in societal and political contexts. Evidence-based policy-making implies that policy-makers use the best available evidence to help make policy decisions. Thereby one usually thinks of evidence as scientific evidence. But policy-making is in general based on more than just scientific evidence: it also takes into account societal considerations, such as the values, interests and concerns that live in society. Good or responsible scientific policy advising requires a careful balance between impartially presenting all available scientific evidence, mapping societal contexts and analysing possible interactions between the scientific and the societal domain. This balance, combined with the issue of detecting and dealing with biases, is the central topic of this book.

Having worked for more than 30 years at the intersection of science and policy, I am aware of the tendency of researchers, scientific advisers and policy-makers, of all who are active in the science-policy ecosystem, to be unconscious of their biases and, so, to be self-assured when dealing with evidence. I am also concerned that participants and societal stakeholders might not think enough about the possible societal impacts, intended or otherwise, of techno-scientific developments. With this book, I aim to raise awareness of our cognitive biases, which can influence the quality of our policy advice, and I describe practical approaches to assessing the possible future impacts of techno-scientific developments on all aspects of society. These procedures are based on my own experiences and a study of the literature, and I have tested them over the last several years in my work on scientific foresight at the European Parliament.

I believe that it will benefit scientists, policy advisers and politicians to investigate the shortcomings in our thinking about scientific evidence when we deal with techno-scientific developments and their possible consequences. In addition, I want to motivate policy professionals and citizens to think carefully about how science can best contribute to society.

I have checked the ideas in this book against the practical experiences of 51 interviewees drawn from throughout the science-policy ecosystem: researchers; professors; high-level experts; scientific advisers; policy analysts; politicians; journalists; consultants and managers, including several top officials from various universities, governments and international organizations. The 21 women and 30 men between 26 and 90 years old from 18 countries are listed in Appendix A. I am grateful for having had the opportunity to discuss these issues with these prominent authorities, all of whom agreed that I could integrate their anonymized views into the book. Each contributed to my ideas about bias, the possible impacts of techno-scientific developments, the production and use of scientific evidence and effective and trustworthy scientific policy advice. Besides scrutinising my assumptions, observations and conclusions, they have contributed several illustrative cases. Without their contributions, this book would not have been possible.

The book has five chapters.

In Chapter 1, I approach the science-policy interface holistically by positioning it in and then outlining the science-policy ecosystem, the widest possible system in which science interacts with policy.

The discussion of cognitive biases in Chapter 2 will help scientific advisers and the policy-makers they advise to be on the alert for them. It synopsises biases in a bias wheel, which I designed as a tool for raising bias awareness.

Chapter 3's focus is on practical, tested ways to conduct scientific foresight that will help scientific advisers to support policy-makers' efforts to be prepared for the future. A central element in this chapter is the STEEPED scheme, which I recommend as a tool for ensuring that one investigates a policy issue from all possible perspectives.

In Chapter 4, I describe systems thinking practices for scientific advisory projects, while focusing on cross-policy impacts. I describe structured ways for advisers to conduct cross-policy analyses, so as to avoid policy actions that will be regretted later. They include a framework for identifying policies associated with the issue investigated and a practical tool, namely, a doughnut scheme, for assessing cross-policy impacts and anticipating unwanted effects.

In these four chapters, I supplement my experience in scientific advising, foresight and communication with recent research into bias in scientific advisory processes in order to devise best practices for scientific advisers, which are intended to support them in being aware of bias and, so, as impartial as possible in conducting transparent, well-designed and inclusive advisory processes that take the possible social impacts of techno-scientific developments into account.

Chapter 5 summarises the practical steps I advocated in earlier chapters towards offering what I call 'Responsible Scientific Advice' to policy-makers. It covers guidelines for communication to audiences with diverse levels of background knowledge and involvement in the issue. It also focuses on the trustworthiness of various players in the science-policy ecosystem.

The book is illustrated with real and hypothetical cases to stimulate reflection on the part of science-policy professionals and engaged citizens.

Overall, with this book I hope to offer a practical framework for supporting scientific advisers in generating sound policy advice. For policy-makers, I hope this book will help them in critically employing scientific evidence and scientific advice, by giving them hands-on tools for investigating possible unintended impacts of their policy choices, so as to avoid actions that will be regretted later. Especially, I hope the tools offered will help them to be well prepared for future societal challenges.

CONTENTS

1 Scientific Policy Advising: Exploring the Science-Policy
   Ecosystem   1

2 How Bias Distorts Evidence and Its Assessment   17

3 Scientific Foresight: Considering the Future of Science
   and Technology   39

4 Systems Thinking and Assessing Cross-Policy Impacts   69

5 Towards Responsible Scientific Advice: Painting
   the Complete Picture   85

Conclusion: Scientific Policy Advice Beyond the Evidence   115

Appendix A: Interviewees   119

Appendix B: Additional Readings   123

Index   125

ABOUT THE AUTHOR

Lieve Van Woensel is Head of Service at the European Parliament, where she introduced foresight methodologies into scientific advisory processes. She has a broad scientific background, has worked for over 30 years at the science-policy interface and was the EU Visiting Fellow at St Antony's College, University of Oxford, 2017–2018. url: https://lievevanwoensel.com.

ABBREVIATIONS

CCS	Carbon Capture and Storage
CSA	Chief Scientific Adviser
CSaP	Centre for Science and Policy, Cambridge University
DBT	Danish Board of Technology
EC	European Commission
EEA	European Environment Agency
EFSA	European Food Safety Authority
EP	European Parliament
EPRS	European Parliamentary Research Service
EPTA	European Parliamentary Technology Assessment
ESA	European Space Agency
ESAF	European Science Advisors Forum
EU	European Union
FAO	Food and Agriculture Organization
GM	Genetically Modified
GMC	General Medical Council, UK
IEA	International Energy Agency
INGSA	International Network for Government Science Advice
IPCC	Intergovernmental Panel on Climate Change
ITA	Institute of Technology Assessment, Austria
JRC	Joint Research Centre of the European Commission
KNAW	Royal Netherlands Academy of Arts and Sciences (Koninklijke Nederlandse Academie van Wetenschappen)
MEP	Member of the European Parliament
MMR	Measles, Mumps, Rubella

NASA	National Aeronautics and Space Administration, United States of America
NGO	Non-Governmental Organization
NTB	Norwegian Board of Technology
OAW	Austrian Academy of Sciences
OECD	Organization for Economic Co-operation and Development
OPECST	Parliamentary Office for Scientific and Technological Assessment, France (Office Parlementaire d'Evaluation des Choix Scientifiques et Technologiques)
PNS	Post-Normal Science
POST	Parliamentary Office of Science and Technology
RRI	Responsible Research and Innovation
RSA	Responsible Scientific Advice
RTDI	Research, Technological Development and Innovation
SAGE	Scientific Advisory Group for Emergencies
SAM	Scientific Advice Mechanism
SDGs	Sustainable Development Goals
STEaPP	Department of Science, Technology, Engineering and Public Policy, University College, London
STOA	European Parliament's Panel for the Future of Science and Technology (former Science and Technology Options Assessment Panel)
TA	Technology Assessment
TA-SWISS	Swiss Foundation for Technology Assessment
TAB	Office of Technology Assessment, Germany
TAMI	Technology Assessment in Europe Between Method and Impact
UN	United Nations
WRR	Scientific Council for Government Policy, Netherlands (Wetenschappelijke Raad voor het Regeringsbeleid)

LIST OF FIGURES

Fig. 1.1   Actors in two simple science-policy interfaces   10
Fig. 1.2   The basic science-policy ecosystem   13
Fig. 1.3   The science-policy ecosystem and external influences
            on its actors   14
Fig. 2.1   The bias wheel: a tool for becoming aware of biases
            in scientific advising   33
Fig. 3.1   World map projection with the North Pole in the centre,
            Rigobert Bonne, 1780   49
Fig. 3.2   World map projection with the South Pole in the centre,
            Rigobert Bonne, 1780   50
Fig. 3.3   The STEEPED scheme   51
Fig. 3.4   The STEEPED scheme with all of its areas   56
Fig. 4.1   The Sustainable Development Goals set by the United Nations   72
Fig. 4.2   The doughnut scheme for assessing possible cross-policy
            impacts   79
Fig. 4.3   A scenario of a new way of living adapted to climate change
            and a higher sea level, *Floating community on the ocean
            with floating farm and floating energy production
            (Artist: Peter Van Woensel)*   82
Fig. 5.1   The science-policy ecosystem's components relevant
            for scientific advisers   87
Fig. 5.2   Foresight shifting participants' concerns
            to wider times and spaces   95
Fig. 5.3   Communication formats for scientific advice   98
Fig. 5.4   Steps and tools in a typical foresight-based scientific
            advisory project   101

LIST OF BOXES

Box 3.1   Steps and timeline of a STOA scientific foresight study   64
Box 4.1   The 17 Sustainable Development Goals adopted
          by the United Nations in 2015   73
Box 4.2   List of the European Parliament's competences   77

CHAPTER 1

Scientific Policy Advising: Exploring the Science-Policy Ecosystem

Abstract People usually suppose that policy is evidence-based. However, democratic decision-making requires a cautious balance between scientific evidence and other inputs, such as citizens' voices. This chapter explains some of the aims and forms of scientific policy advice and considers some of the roles that scientific policy advisers can play. It describes the science-policy ecosystem holistically to explain the scientific and other inputs to scientific policy advice and other factors that can influence the scientific advisory process.

Keywords Evidence-based policy-making · Scientific advice · Science-policy ecosystem · Scientific foresight · Systems analysis

In this chapter, I describe the science-policy ecosystem. I first explain some of the aims and forms of scientific advising. Second, I explain some advising practices, including some of the good practices that well-known advisers have published. Next, I consider the roles that scientific advisers can play. I then zoom out from the scientific advice process in the simplest science-policy interface to a systems analysis of the more complicated science-policy ecosystem. Finally, I consider some possible distracting influences in the ecosystem of which scientific advisers should be aware.

L. Van Woensel, *A Bias Radar for Responsible Policy-Making*, St Antony's Series, https://doi.org/10.1007/978-3-030-32126-0_1

1.1   Issues for Which Policy-Makers Need Advice

Governmental and parliamentary policy-makers usually need scientific advice on a specific development, problem or trend, for example:

- What are criteria of trustworthiness for a certain algorithm?
- How might a new technology impact the labour market?
- How can food waste be cut?
- How can we mitigate, and reverse, plastic pollution?
- How can the effects of fake news (and other forms of disinformation) be minimized?
- What are the possible global threats of artificial intelligence, and how can they be countered?
- What are the technological options for exploring and exploiting the deep seabed?

But they must also make strategic policy decisions to anticipate a more general challenge, threat or trend. Examples requiring scientific advice are:

- How can we ensure food resilience?
- How can we prepare for a rise in the sea level?
- How can we anticipate and manage immigration crises so that they do not overwhelm social resources?
- Which ethical implications may require limitations to human enhancement by gene editing technologies?

So, the range of issues for which policy-makers need scientific advice includes technological, behavioural and ethical matters arising across the spectrum of political competences: energy, transportation, the environment, public health, the digital revolution, employment, agriculture and climate change. This book's approach to policy advising applies to all of these subjects.

1.2   Scientific Advising: Criteria, Organizations and Practices

In this sub-section, I first consider some of the organizational criteria for scientific policy advising that are described in some prominent reviews of the broad literature on the subject, and I explain some actual advising structures. Next, I survey some of the good practices of some well-known advisers. Appendix B lists references for further reading.

1.2.1 Organizational Criteria for Effective, Trustworthy and High-Quality Advising

In its report *Scientific Advice for Policy Making: The Role and Responsibility of Expert Bodies and Individual Scientists*, the Organization for Economic Co-operation and Development (OECD 2015) analyses the organization of scientific policy advising and recommends three criteria for effective and trustworthy advising:

1. Have a clear remit, with defined roles and responsibilities for the various actors;
2. Involve scientists, policy-makers and other stakeholders in the process only when their input is relevant;
3. Provide advice that is sound, unbiased and legitimate.

In *The Politics of Scientific Advice: Institutional Design for Quality Assurance*, Justus Lentsch and Peter Weingart (2011) also explore the institutional design of advisory organisations and how it affects their ability to meet the challenges of policy advising. They derive four organizational guidelines for ensuring the quality of advice:

1. Maintain distance between advisers and advised to safeguard the former's independence;
2. Involve different disciplines in the advisory process to ensure a plurality of perspectives;
3. Establish trust by maintaining transparent procedures;
4. Ensure public access to all relevant information.

1.2.2 How Scientific Advising Is Organized

National governments and legislatures and international legislative bodies have established a variety of institutional structures for generating scientific advice. In this subsection, I describe two models and consider some examples to illustrate how scientific policy advising can be organised. However, I do not provide an exhaustive list of models or scientific policy advising bodies.

National governments and legislatures and international legislative bodies have established a variety of institutional structures for generating scientific advice. The two most common structures are the Chief Scientific Adviser (CSA) and the parliamentary or governmental scientific advisory body or committee. A CSA's task is to provide governments and their departments with strategic and operational scientific advice on questions pertaining to science policy. The CSA model is typical for Anglo-Saxon countries, and in recent years several have appointed them. The US appointed its CSA, the world's first, in 1957 followed by the UK in 1964 and Ireland in 2004. In 2009, New Zealand appointed its first CSA, and in 2011 Quebec appointed the first CSA in Canada. In 2012, the European Commission appointed Anne Glover as the first CSA to the President of the European Commission. But her role was never clearly defined, she was under-funded and she worked as part of the Barroso Commission, whose mandate ended in October 2014, and her office was abolished that year. A polarizing debate ensued over whether the European Commission needed a CSA or an advisory body with members covering different disciplines. Eventually, the Juncker Commission decided on the latter and established the Scientific Advice Mechanism (SAM), a body of seven prominent scientists from various disciplines, which has advised the College of European Commissioners since the end of 2015. SAM provides the Commission with high-quality, timely and independent scientific policy advice.

Scientific advisory bodies usually serve parliaments, though a few also advise governments and their ministries. Overall, technology assessment (TA) bodies, which are the common scientific advisory bodies for public policy, can be quite varied. They can be based within the parliamentary administration or a ministry or be an independent organisation. Their tasks can range from informing only the parliament to stimulating public debate. Some conduct TAs using own expertise; others partly or primarily outsource their TA studies.

One example of a parliamentary advisory body is the European Parliament's Panel for the Future of Science and Technology (STOA). Established in 1987, it is administered by the EP's secretariat. 25 Members of the European Parliament, who are nominated by nine parliamentary committees, now sit on the panel. STOA is part of the Scientific Foresight

Unit, which is embedded in the European Parliamentary Research Service (EPRS), the EP's think tank. STOA's mission is 'to contribute to the debate on and the legislative consideration of scientific and technological issues of particular political relevance.'[1] Another prominent example is Finland's Committee for the Future, established in 1993, which has the mission of generating parliamentary dialogue on major future problems and opportunities. It is a permanent committee of 17 parliamentarians drawn from all of the political parties represented in the parliament, and they deliberate about matters affecting future research, technology and its impacts. In effect, they act as Finland's think tank and guard against parliamentary and government short-sightedness. Other European examples (some of which also advise other governmental bodies) are:

- France's *Office Parlementaire d'Evaluation des Choix Scientifiques et Technologiques* (the Parliamentary Office for Evaluation of Scientific and Technological Options) (OPECST), created in 1983;
- The Institute of Technology Assessment (ITA) of the Austrian Academy of Sciences (OAW), founded in 1994;
- The UK's Parliamentary Office of Science and Technology (POST), launched in 1989;
- The Office of Technology Assessment (TAB), created in 1990, an independent scientific institution advising the German parliament;
- The Rathenau Institute, founded in 1986, an independent organisation for research and dialogue that falls under the administrative responsibility of the Royal Netherlands Academy of Arts and Sciences (KNAW);
- The Norwegian Board of Technology (NTB), an independent TA body that advises the Norwegian parliament and other governmental bodies, established in 1999;
- The Swiss Foundation for Technology Assessment (TA-SWISS), which has advised the Swiss parliament since 1991;
- The Danish Board of Technology (DBT), established by the Danish parliament as an independent body in 1986 and now a foundation, it has been a pioneer in technology assessment and foresight.

---

[1] http://www.europarl.europa.eu/stoa/.

The number of scientists serving on these parliamentary scientific advisory bodies varies from a few to over fifty, including experts in a wide range of disciplines. Most have a board comprised of members of parliament.

A prominent example of a governmental scientific advisory organisation is the Netherlands' Scientific Council for Government Policy (WRR). Established in 1976, the WWR[2] is an independent body that advises the Dutch government on strategic policy issues that are of great importance for society. The Council's members conduct its projects though external scientists participate occasionally.

In most cases, parliamentary and governmental scientific advisory services include their reports external inputs, from academies of science and individual or groups of academics or consultants, though they are always in control of the process and responsible for its outcomes.

Nowadays, scientific advising is itself a subject of research, and researchers compare different countries' models and practices. For instance, the Centre for Science and Policy (CSaP) at the University of Cambridge, UK, promotes relationships between policy professionals and scientists and engineers. The CSaP works with a network of academics and decision-makers to improve the use of evidence and of expertise in public policy, and it plays an important role in governmental science advising in Europe and around the world.

Governmental and parliamentary science advisers all over the world have established networks to discuss their experiences. Two examples are the European Science Advisors Forum (ESAF) and the International Network for Government Science Advice (INGSA). The ESAF is an independent, informal network of European strategic scientific advisers, whose members are nominated by EU-member governments at the request of the European Commission. It began as a 'forum of EU member-countries' science advisers with a formal and active position to provide science-based strategic advice to their democratic governments'.[3] The INGSA provides a forum for policy-makers and practitioners, national academies, scientific societies and researchers to share their experiences and develop theoretical and practical approaches to the use of scientific evidence in policies at all levels of government.

---

[2] https://english.wrr.nl/.

[3] https://esaforum.eu.

The European Parliamentary Technology Assessment (EPTA)[4] is a network of TA institutions that specialise in advising European parliaments. Its partners advise numerous parliaments on the possible social, economic and environmental impact of new sciences and technologies. A selection of the members has been described above in this section.

The mission of these networks is to exchange information and good practices and share advice with governments concerning governance and policy.

1.2.3   Good Scientific Advising Practices

Key people in the scientific advising business have the good habit of sharing their successful practices. In his paper 'The Art of Science Advice to Government' (Gluckman 2014), Peter Gluckman, New Zealand's first CSA, states 10 principles, four of which are relevant here. He starts with maintaining trust. Scientific advisers need to maintain the trust of many—the public, the media, policy-makers, politicians and the science community— and Gluckman's first principle is that advisers clearly communicate what they know, what they are uncertain about and what they do not know. His second principle is that the head of government receive the advice directly from advisers to prevent its being censored by department or ministry heads. Third is to distinguish scientific policy advice from advice on science policy and the administration of public funding for science. If one entity does both, there is a conflict of interest and a consequent loss of trust. The fourth principle is that advisers do not make policy. They gather and analyse the scientific evidence. Deciding on policy involves choosing from policy options with different trade-offs among social costs and benefits, and that choice should not rest with the scientific advisers but with the policy-makers, either elected politicians or those they appoint to draft policy.

Another adviser who shares his successful practices is Chris Tyler, who spent five years as Director of the UK's Parliamentary Office of Science and Technology (POST) and today is Director of Public Policy in the Department of Science, Technology, Engineering and Public Policy (STEaPP) at University College London. In 'Three Secrets of Survival in Science Advice'

---

[4] https://eptanetwork.org/.

(Tyler and Akerlof 2019), he and Karen Akerlof recommend three principles for legislative scientific advisers to follow to survive changes in legislators: maintain political neutrality among legislative factions, choose policy advising over taking sides in controversies and give value for the money. Two STOA colleagues and I added a fourth recommendation to incorporate an internal source of strategic advice for providing the facts needed to resolve difficult arguments in negotiations (Quaglio et al. 2019). Regarding Tyler and Akerhof's recommendation on neutrality, I have learned from my interviewees that parliamentary and governmental advisers generally try to be honest brokers, especially when dealing with uncertain or controversial issues. I explain the concept of the honest broker (Pielke 2007) in Section 1.3 below. Here I only need to say that an honest broker helps policy-makers choose wisely from among available policy options, and that demands political neutrality. More specifically, appropriate advice on a policy question has to reflect the range of opinion in the science community and the interests of stakeholders (see Chapter 3). In practice, then, there is no uniquely best policy. Rather, advisers compile a set of policy options that jointly constitute their recommendation. And parliamentary advisers work for all of the parliament's factions, not just the ruling majority; so, they have to be politically neutral in compiling options.

William Sutherland, Sir David Spiegelhalter and Marc Brugman published 'Twenty Tips for Interpreting Scientific Claims' in 2013 (Sutherland et al. 2013). One of their tips is 'Scientists are human', i.e., 'Scientists have a vested interest in promoting their work… This can lead to selective reporting of results and, occasionally, exaggeration. … Multiple, independent sources of evidence are much more convincing.' Another tip is 'Feelings influence risk perception'. (In Chapter 2, I discuss bias and how it distorts our perception of evidence.)

Christl A. Donnelly, a Fellow of the Royal Society (UK), and her co-authors argue in 'Four Principles to Make Evidence Synthesis more Useful for Policy' (Donnelly et al. 2018) that an accurate, concise and unbiased synthesis of the available scientific evidence is one of the most valuable kinds of help that advisers can offer policy-makers. And they recommend that advisers rephrase policy-makers' common question "What is the evidence for that?" as the more useful "Has all of the available evidence relating to that been sufficiently synthesized?" They state four principles for advisers to make their syntheses of scientific evidence as useful to policy-makers as possible: syntheses should be inclusive, rigorous, transparent and accessible. As they explain, a synthesis is inclusive when it covers many types and sources of evidence and a range of experts employing a variety of methods have contributed to it. A rigorous synthesis incorporates the most comprehensive body of evidence feasible; it minimizes bias, and it is independently reviewed in a quality-assurance process. A transparent synthesis clearly formulates the research question (see Chapter 5) and describes the research methods, sources of evidence and quality-assurance process; it describes any complications and areas of contention; it makes explicit its assumptions, limitations and uncertainties, including any gaps in the evidence, and it declares all personal, political and organisational interests and resolves any conflicts among them. An accessible synthesis is written in clear language; it is available within a reasonable timeframe and it is freely available online.

The preceding principles set the right tone for understanding the practical framework for scientific policy advising that I propose below.

1.2.4 Evidence-Based Policy-Making: A Reflection on Rationality and Other Values

Before I proceed, I want briefly to clarify an issue: How strictly evidence-based should policy-making be in a democracy?

"Evidence-based policy-making" refers to deciding policy entirely on the basis of scientific evidence, and that approach assumes that scientific evidence is value-free and, so, best serves society's needs. But policy based exclusively on scientific evidence is technocratic, which is not the aim of policy in a democracy. Democratic policy-makers combine the best available evidence with their understanding of society's needs. What we can call "evidence-informed policy-making" uses the best available scientific evidence but contextualizes it in terms of what policy-makers believe accords with citizens' expectations, values and preferences.

Berry Tholen argues in *Virtue and Responsibility in Policy Research and Advice* (Tholen 2017) that, though the work of scientists should be value-neutral, democratic politicians should not be confined to such technocratic ways of thinking. It is entirely legitimate for them to take their ideologies and cultural preferences into account. Along the same lines, Paul Cairney explains in *The Politics of Evidence-Based Policy Making* (2016) that policy-makers make decisions both rationally and non-rationally. Rationally, they make policy decisions on the basis of the evidence; non-rationally, they allow themselves to be influenced by emotions and beliefs informed by them. (In Chapter 3, I describe an approach to policy advising that includes both by combining scientific evidence and societal context.)

1.3   The Roles that Scientific Advisers Can Play

Scientific advisers must be aware of the diverse roles they can play. In *The Honest Broker: Making Sense of Science in Policy and Politics* (Pielke 2007), Roger Pielke describes various roles in which advisers can engage with policy and politics. Two of these are 'science arbitration' and 'honest brokering of policy alternatives'. The science arbiter advises policy-makers by using the tools of science to answer their empirical questions. This role fits the simple linear models of the science-policy interface illustrated in Fig. 1.1. They represent the flow of knowledge from scientific research to policy decisions that is characteristic of evidence-based policy-making. The honest broker's role is more complex. The honest broker formulates a range of evidence-informed policy options, which integrate the scientific evidence with policy stakeholders' concerns, so as to empower policy-makers. Pielke calls this non-linear science-policy interface the "stakeholder model". All of my recommendations for policy advisers are based on this stakeholder model. Honest brokering is a role that only advisory bodies can play, for it is impossible for an individual adviser to have expertise in enough areas to be able to recommend a range of policy alternatives each of which is supported by the scientific evidence.

As I said above, parliamentary advisers, like we in STOA, tend to be honest brokers. So, their advice on a policy question has to reflect the range of opinion in the science community and among stakeholders. So, it must be based on considerations of the scientific evidence in the relevant societal contexts. Consequently, there is no uniquely best policy. But they cannot formulate for policy-makers' consideration all of the options that are technologically possible. So, the adviser's job is to assess the technical

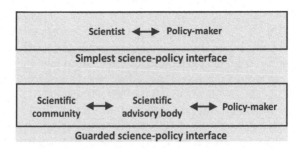

Fig. 1.1   Actors in two simple science-policy interfaces

and social feasibility of what is possible and formulate the feasible options as their recommendation to policy-makers.

The honest broker is the most impartial and trustworthy role that advisers can play. (In Chapter 3, I explain how foresight helps them to avoid being science arbiters by making them articulate the possible effects of policy options on stakeholders.)

1.4   The Science-Policy Ecosystem: Zooming Out to the Whole Picture

1.4.1   Simple Science-Policy Interfaces

The simplest connection between science and policy is the direct interface between scientists and policy-makers. In another simple interface, scientific advisers mediate between the two (see Fig. 1.1).

1.4.2   The Science-Policy Ecosystem: A Holistic Approach to Advising

In this sub-section, I explain the elements of an ideal scientific advisory process by locating it in what I call the "science-policy ecosystem", which includes more than the scientific community and policy-makers. To introduce it, I zoom out from a hypothetical example of an issue for which policy-makers seek advice, describing the ecosystem's actors and inputs as I go.

The scientific advisory process starts with advisers investigating the needs that prompted the policy-makers' question. Once they grasp the issue, advisers plan how they will proceed. To draw up their plan, advisers must consider the sources of input to their research into the question; the stakeholders, i.e., those who are affected by or who can affect the policy issue, and the relevant institutional memory, among other things.

1.4.3   A Hypothetical Problem

Suppose that policy-makers ask, "**How can food waste be cut?**" Six subsidiary questions immediately arise:

- **Who** wastes food? Citizens? Food industries? Supermarkets?
- **What** is food waste exactly? Does it include peelings, bones, skins and shells?

- **Where** is food wasted? In households? In restaurants? On which geographical area should advisers focus?
- **When** is food wasted? Does it happen seasonally? Is it due to unanticipated oversupplies?
- **Why** is food wasted? Do citizens buy too much? Do restaurants and catering services provide too much? Are people confused about "best before" and "use by" dates? Do they fear health risks in eating food after the expiration date? Are they hesitant to buy fruits and vegetables that do not look perfect?
- **How** can the identified sources of food waste be avoided? What regulations, for instance, about food safety, already exist? What novel measures are possible?

These six guiding questions expand what first seemed like a simple problem. And they reveal that some food waste might be driven by emotions, such as consumers' fears about the safety of food after the "best before" date, their preference for perfect fruit or their refusal to adapt their diet to what is in greatest supply at the moment.

Once they have the full picture, advisers must plan the inputs to their research:

- the scientific input;
- stakeholders' views on the issue and their role in food waste;
- an overview of existing regulations on food waste.

Now the real scientific advisory work begins. Advisers synthesise all of the scientific evidence; investigate the issue's full societal context, which includes farmers, retailers, consumers, the food industry, waste management services and other stakeholders; analyse all the information they collect and formulate and assess policy options.

However, before advisers report their findings to policy-makers, they must address another issue: Do their recommended policy options affect other policies (for agriculture, consumer affairs, public health, development, the environment or trade)? To do so, they must zoom out from the policy-makers' issue to the broadest view of the science-policy ecosystem. In this way, their work is holistic. We can employ systems theory to visualise an all-embracing science-policy ecosystem.

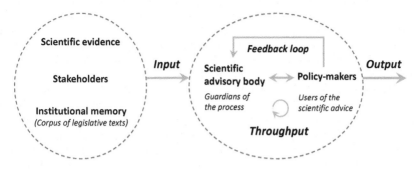

Fig. 1.2 The basic science-policy ecosystem

Inspired by the work of systems analysts (Ashby 1960; Brown et al. 2017; Luhmann 1995; Meadows and Wright 2008; Schaveling and Bryan 2018; Senge 2006; Vickers 1965), I initially conceived the science-policy ecosystem as including the elements illustrated in Fig. 1.2. So conceived, the ecosystem includes (i) the interaction with policy-makers; (ii) the required types of input (scientific evidence, stakeholders' views and the relevant institutional memory); (iii) what systems theory calls the "throughput", which consists in the analysis of the input within the frame of the policy-makers' original question; (iv) the feedback loop from policy-makers to advisers through which the latter ensure that the former have received an adequate answer to their question and (v) the output of the ecosystem, *viz.*, the policy decision.

However, according to Luhmann's systems theory the basic ecosystem is an 'open system', i.e., one that can exchange information with its surroundings, and I wanted to incorporate this. All of the actors in the scientific advisory process—scientists, advisers, policy-makers and stakeholders—can be biased by influences like their personal environments, interest groups and the media. Figure 1.3 makes this explicit by including outside influences on different parts of the ecosystem.

Understanding the ecosystem sheds light on the influences at work in the advisory process. Advisers are the guardians of the proper functioning and integrity of the advisory process. They must provide policy-makers the advice they need; manage outside influences and ensure the quality of the input, throughput and their final recommendations.

In sum, the full science-policy ecosystem has the following constituents:

- Policy-makers;
- Scientific advisers;
- The scientific community;
- Societal stakeholders;
- Special-interest and pressure groups;
- The media;

all of whom can be influenced or deceived by biases. The ecosystem also includes the personal environment of every actor because this influences their views.

1.4.4   Distracting Influences in the Science-Policy Ecosystem

As Fig. 1.3 shows, inputs to the scientific advisory process do not come only from the scientific community; other factors influence scientists, advisers and policy-makers, including some that affect public opinion and seek to influence policy. These factors include players' personal environments, the mainstream and social media, interest groups and what Roger Pielke (Pielke 2007) describes as "Stealth Issue Advocates", i.e., experts skilful at confusing issues for policy-makers, citizens and even scientists. In their book *Merchants of Doubt: How a Handful of Scientists Obscured the Truth on Issues from Tobacco Smoke to Global Warming* (Oreskes and Conway 2010),

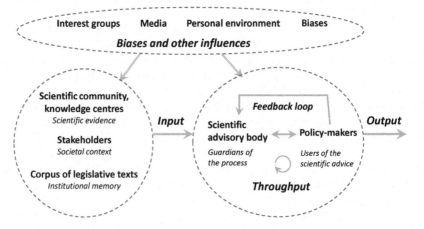

Fig. 1.3   The science-policy ecosystem and external influences on its actors

Naomi Oreskes and Erik Conway call them "merchants of doubt" and describe how they run effective campaigns to cast doubt on well-established scientific knowledge in order to mislead the public (see Chapter 2). In effect, all of these factors are uncontrolled sources of input to the advisory process, and scientific advisers must be aware of them.

In addition to these, cognitive bias, which affects everyone, is an uncontrolled influence acting throughout the policy advising process, and it can lead to prejudiced or partisan scientific advice. (This is the subject of Chapter 2.)

1.5   Chapter Summary and Conclusions

Scientific policy advising usually pertains to policy problems involving new technology. It can be organized as a CSA or an advisory body. Scientific policy advice should be sound, unbiased, legitimate and publicly accessible. In addition to scientists, scientific advisers should consult stakeholders in a policy issue. They should work as honest brokers, formulating for policy-makers' consideration a set of politically neutral policy options.

To ensure that their approach is holistic and their advice is all-encompassing, advisers should begin with a systems analysis. To analyse a policy problem systematically, advisers should broaden it by asking six guiding questions: Who?, What?, Where?, When?, Why? and How?

In the ideal science-policy ecosystem, scientific advisers can identify all of the factors they may have to consider in the course of a scientific advisory project and some possible distracting external influences that can affect public opinions and influence policy.

Scientific advisers are the guardians of the advisory process, and it is their responsibility to ensure that their policy advice is impartial and useful.

References

Ashby, W. Ross. 1960. *Design for a Brain: The Origin of Adaptive Behavior.* 2nd, rev. ed. London: Chapman & Hall.

Brown, Andrew W., Tapan S. Mehta, and David B. Allison. 2017. "Publication Bias in Science: What Is It, Why Is It Problematic, and How Can It Be Addressed." In *The Oxford Handbook on the Science of Science Communication,* edited by Kathleen Hall Jamieson, Dan M. Kahan, and Dietram Scheufele, 93–101. New York: Oxford University Press.

Cairney, Paul. 2016. *The Politics of Evidence-Based Policy Making*. London: Palgrave Macmillan.

Donnelly, Christl A., Ian Boyd, Philip Campbell, Claire Craig, Patrick Vallance, Mark Walport, Christopher J. M. Whitty, Emma Woods, and Chris Wormald. 2018. "Four Principles to Make Evidence Synthesis More Useful for Policy." *Nature* 558 (7710): 361. https://doi.org/10.1038/d41586-018-05414-4.

Gluckman, Peter. 2014. "The Art of Science Advice to Government". *Nature* 507 (7491): 163–165.

Lentsch, Justus, and Peter Weingart. 2011. *The Politics of Scientific Advice: Institutional Design for Quality Assurance*. Cambridge: Cambridge University Press.

Luhmann, Niklas. 1995. *Social Systems*. Translated by John Bednarz and Dirk Baecker. Stanford, CA: Stanford University Press. Original edition, Soziale Systeme: Grundriss einer allgemeinen Theorie, 1984.

Meadows, Donella H., and Diana Wright. 2008. *Thinking in Systems: A Primer*. White River Junction, VT: Chelsea Green Publishing.

Organisation for Economic Co-operation and Development (OECD). 2015. "Scientific Advice for Policy Making: The Role and Responsibility of Expert Bodies and Individual Scientists." IDEAS Working Paper Series from RePEc.

Oreskes, Naomi, and Erik M. Conway. 2010. *Merchants of Doubt: How a Handful of Scientists Obscured the Truth on Issues from Tobacco Smoke to Global Warming*. New York: Bloomsbury Press.

Quaglio, Gianluca, Lieve Van Woensel, and Theo Karapiperis. 2019. "Strategic Advice is Crucial for European Policy." *Nature* 569: 455.

Pielke, Roger A. 2007. *The Honest Broker: Making Sense of Science in Policy and Politics*. Cambridge: Cambridge University Press.

Schaveling, Jaap, and Bill Bryan. 2018. *Making Better Decisions Using Systems Thinking: How to Stop Firefighting, Deal with Root Causes and Deliver Permanent Solutions*. Switzerland: Palgrave Macmillan.

Senge, Peter M. 2006. *The Fifth Discipline: The Art and Practice of the Learning Organization*. Rev. and updated ed. London: Random House Business Books.

Sutherland, William J., David Spiegelhalter, Mark A. Burgman. 2013. "Twenty Tips for Interpreting Scientific Claims." *Nature* 503 (7476), 335–337.

Tholen, Berry. 2017. *Virtue and Responsibility in Policy Research and Advice*. New York, NY: Springer.

Tyler, Chris, and Karen Akerlof. 2019. "Three Secrets of Survival in Science Advice." *Nature* 566: 175.

Vickers, Geoffrey. 1965. *The Art of Judgment: A Study of Policy Making*. London: Chapman & Hall.

CHAPTER 2

How Bias Distorts Evidence and Its Assessment

Abstract Scientific policy advisers collect information and on its basis formulate alternative policy options for policy-makers to consider. Throughout the process, biases can cause systematically distorted perceptions of facts and opinions in virtue of which advisers fail to weigh evidence, assessments and points of view objectively. The chapter first develops a better understanding of unconscious biases, what they are and how they occur. It then introduces the phenomenon of cognitive dissonance, which explains why we are intrinsically biased. Next, it describes and illustrates some well-known and some lesser-known biases. Finally, the chapter proposes the bias wheel as a practical method of checking for bias and promoting bias-awareness.

Keywords Bias · Cognitive dissonance · Bias-awareness · Bias wheel · Critical thinking

This chapter is about the cognitive biases that affect scientific advisers' assessments of evidence. In general, a bias is a mental inclination or disposition in a certain direction. Our thinking is biased when we allow our opinions to influence our conclusions in systematically prejudicial ways, which often results in systematically distorted perceptions of facts and opinions. Thus, bias interferes with critical thinking and, thereby, the rationality of conclusions and decisions. Biases also allow us to make faster decisions

L. Van Woensel, *A Bias Radar for Responsible Policy-Making*,
St Antony's Series, https://doi.org/10.1007/978-3-030-32126-0_2

when confronted with new facts, especially undesirable or inconvenient ones. At the same time, hasty decision-making increases the risk of further bias. Biases throughout the advisory process can cause advisers to fail to weigh evidence, assessments and points of view objectively.

I develop insight into explain unconscious biases and how they occur. I first explain what biases are and the origin of the term and describe some of the early science about them. I then explain cognitive dissonance, which causes us to be intrinsically biased. I also consider when advisors should strive to eliminate bias and when they can live with it. Next, I describe some well-known and lesser-known biases, which I illustrate with three cases. Finally, I summarize a set of biases in the bias wheel, a tool I developed for checking for bias and promoting bias-awareness.

2.1   Bias Basics

2.1.1   Origin of the Word "Bias": Biased Balls in the Old Game of Bowls

Before I dig into biases, I explain the non-cognitive origin of the term "bias". The earliest known reference is in William Fitzstephen's twelfth-century biography of Thomas Becket, the Archbishop of Canterbury, who lived from ca. 1120 until his murder in 1170. In his book (n.d.) Fitzstephen describes lawn bowling as a summer amusement of young men in London that included the use of biased bowls (Wikisource 2019). A biased bowl was weighted on one side so that it would roll along a path curved towards the heavier, or biased, side (History of Bowls, n.d.). Why do I mention this in a book on policy advising? An unbiased bowl's straight path is predictable, but the curved path of a biased one is not always, for its trajectory depends on the amount of its bias (Cross 1998), and, similarly, the outcome of biased thinking is unpredictable when the type of bias, which determines the direction of the distortion, and its extent are not known.

2.1.2   Bias in Nineteenth-Century Sociological Research

The oldest reference to bias in assessing evidence that I have found is that of the polymath Herbert Spencer in *The Study of Sociology* (Spencer 1873). He was probably the first to describe five well-known biases—the educational, patriotism, class, political and theological biases—which he used to illustrate how sociologists' preferences override their background knowledge and the evidence. Spencer also considered methodologies in sociologic research for avoiding them. For instance, to avoid the patriotism bias, which arises from researchers' preferences for their own countries, they should consider the opinions of people from other countries, whose experiences differ from those of their devoted compatriots. More generally, he argued that to avoid biases sociology needed more rigorous research methodologies based on those of the natural sciences.

I mention Spencer to illustrate my thesis that awareness can help us to overcome bias.

2.1.3   How the Brain Biases Thinking

Biases are the results of fast processing in the neural correlates of thinking. In *Thinking Fast and Slow* (Kahneman 2012), Daniel Kahneman describes the brain's main cognitive processes in terms of two interacting systems. System 1, the fast system, is for intuitive and automatic thinking, while the slower System 2 is for thinking that requires attention and mental effort. When System 1 encounters a problem, the brain can switch to System 2, and one thinks more carefully. However, as Kahneman explains, we are innately mentally lazy. In accordance with the law of least effort, we tend to think in ways that need the least amount of energy. The law and the fact that System 2 requires considerably more energy make System 1's intuitive thinking (thinking fast) dominate. In *Brain Chains* (Compernolle 2014), Theo Compernolle calls the neural correlates of intuitive thinking the "reflex brain" and those of explicitly logical, analytical, synthetic and future-oriented thinking (among other forms) the "reflecting brain", which is therefore also the 'goal-oriented brain'. Both authors agree that judgments and decisions are often irrational. So, biases arise from System 1 or the reflex brain more often than from System 2 or the reflecting brain.

Assuming that these theories are approximately true, it seems clear that if we want to get scientific advisers and policy-makers to avoid bias by increasing their awareness of it, we should find ways to induce them to think reflectively. However, reflective thinking requires a lot of energy. So, even if we find such ways, it is not clear that advisers and decision-makers will follow them.

Moreover, neither theory implies that reflective thinking (thinking slow) is always rational. As Hugo Mercier and Dan Sperber explain in their book *The Enigma of Reason* (Mercier and Sperber 2017), reflective thinking is not always dedicated to logical analysis; one also thinks reflectively in trying to defend one's view by looking for arguments that intuitively seem to support it. They take such argumentative thinking to be another system of the goal-oriented brain.

2.2   Cognitive Dissonance

> Cognitive dissonance is the discomfort that people feel when two cognitions (beliefs, attitudes) conflict, or when they behave in ways that are inconsistent with their conception of themselves.—Aronson et al. (2018)

Cognitive dissonance is a psychological phenomenon that induces biased thinking. As Festinger (1957) explained, cognitive dissonance is the uneasiness that one feels when one's actions are contrary to one's beliefs. But, according to Festinger's principle of cognitive consistency, one has an inner drive to keep one's beliefs and behaviour in harmony. So, one must do something, like alter one's set of beliefs, to lessen the inconsistency and the cognitive dissonance it causes.

For instance, Zoe believes that smoking causes cancer, and she intends to quit today. However, she is desperate for a cigarette and, in the end, smokes one. Her action is in conflict with her belief, and she feels the resulting distress of cognitive dissonance. To eliminate it, she must reject or revise her belief or acquire one that lessens or eliminates the inconsistency. Learning that her grandfather, who has just celebrated his 100th birthday, has smoked all his life, she rejects the belief that smoking causes cancer.

2.3   Overcoming Bias or Living with It?

It is accepted as best practice that scientific advisers be what Roger Pielke calls "honest brokers" in *The Honest Broker: Making Sense of Science in Policy and Politics* (Pielke 2007), explaining, '[t]he honest broker of policy alternatives seeks to integrate scientific knowledge with stakeholder concerns in the form of alternative possible courses of action'. So, scientific advisers should be as unbiased as possible in assessing the scientific and societal evidence and formulating policy options on its basis.

On the other hand, policy-makers, who choose from among these options those that best meet their policy goals, should take their own and their constituents' opinions into account when deciding policy. In fact, as Berry Tholen argues in *Virtue and Responsibility in Policy Research and Advice* (Tholen 2017), their role as elected decision-makers demands this.

2.4   THE MOST FREQUENT BIASES IN THE SCIENTIFIC ADVISORY PROCESS

Searching the Internet, one sees that there are dozens of biases, many of which are relevant to dealing with scientific evidence and policy. I first explain what I call "research bias". Next, I describe five other categories of biases that affect advisers' and policy-makers' assessments of evidence and, thus, the decisions they make on its basis. I identify "culture and value biases", "attention biases", "interest biases", "availability biases" and "associative biases". Finally, I arrange these biases into the bias wheel, a tool to enhance the bias-awareness of scientists, scientific advisers, policy-makers and every individual who wants to sharpen his or her critical thinking.

2.4.1   Research Biases

If you torture the data long enough, it will confess to anything.—Huff (1954)

By "research biases", I refer to biases that affect the generation of evidence or its availability. In her paper 'Bias in Research' (Šimundić 2013), Ana-Maria Šimundić explains that biased evidence is the result of 'any trend or deviation from the truth in data collection, data analysis, interpretation and publication, which can cause false conclusions.' Research biases can occur during the sampling and in drawing the conclusions, as the scientists conducting the research can influence its results. Biased evidence can harm the research enterprise, the economy and, in extreme cases, like the Wakefield case described below, human life.

2.4.1.1   Sampling Biases

Sampling biases develop when researchers collect non-representative information. They can be built into data-collection methods that, for example, systematically exclude certain kinds of individuals from a study. If, for instance, you conduct an online survey to collect data on the accessibility of certain information, your sample will fail to represent the part of the population that has not gone digital. Another example that used to be typical of clinical research was the exclusion of women from sample populations so as not to risk harming the foetuses of subjects who become pregnant during a study (Keville 1994). Age and ethnic biases operate similarly. Sampling biases also affect samples that are too small.

2.4.1.2   Experimenter Biases

Experimenter biases are a class of research bias that occur in the design of experiments and the analysis of experimental data, which can lead to biased evidence and conclusions. For instance, research might be built on misleadingly worded questions. A well-known example is the experimenter-expectancy bias, in which experimenters explain experiments data in their research findings incorrectly because of the tendency to pay more attention to information that confirms one's hypotheses and overlook information that disconfirms them (Goldstein 2011). A double-blind experimental design reduces this threat to a study's validity.

Another experimenter bias occurs when researchers interpret their experimental data in ways that enhance the significance of the data that support their hypotheses. This bias often occurs when observed correlations are statistically insignificant. In his 'Address of the President' to the Royal Statistical Society in June 2017 (Spiegelhalter 2017), Sir David Spiegelhalter described the irreproducibility of research results as one of the problems that biased data cause in research.

2.4.1.3   Reporting Biases

Reporting biases are located on the borderline of research biases and those that influence people's assessment of evidence. Reporting biases that affect scientific evidence at the research end lead to availability biases for users of the evidence.

I distinguish two kinds of reporting bias. The first one occurs in researchers' submissions to publishers and the other in the publication process. First, researchers are less likely to submit null results (which do not support their hypotheses) and more likely to submit results for which they have overwhelming evidence. Second, peer reviewers are more likely to accept studies with well-confirmed results, and they are more likely to accept the work of renowned scientists and those from distinguished institutions than that of unknown researchers, which is the Matthew effect. And scientific journals are much more likely to publish a study with positive findings than one with negative findings (Šimundić 2013).

The costs of publication also tend to prevent researchers from submitting and publishers from publishing less interesting results.

2.4.1.4   Sponsorship Bias

The last research bias that I shall mention is the funding or sponsorship bias, which is the tendency of researchers to interpret or manipulate their experimental data so that their results support the interests of their financial sponsors. Sheldon Krimsky (2013) found evidence of the sponsorship bias in his investigation of research into toxic chemicals, tobacco and pharmaceuticals.

2.4.2   Cultural and Value Biases

The first group of assessment biases are cultural and value biases, which include ideological biases, the in-group bias, the confirmation bias and the stereotype bias.

2.4.2.1   The Ideological Bias
The ideological bias occurs when one's religious, cultural or political beliefs affect the objectivity of one's assessment of evidence. Biases can be religious, cultural or political. Because they must be impartial, scientific advisers must avoid the ideological bias, but the same is not true for policy-makers.

2.4.2.2   The In-Group Bias
An in-group is a social group of which one is a member or with which one identifies, and the in-group bias is the tendency to favour evidence that supports the interests of one's in-group (Aronson et al. 2018). The in-group bias is related to group-think, a psychological phenomenon that occurs in a group whose members' desire for harmony or conformity with the group results in irrational or dysfunctional decision-making (Turner and Pratkanis 1998).

2.4.2.3   The Confirmation Bias
The confirmation bias is the tendency to favour or selectively seek out information that confirms one's values, beliefs or hypotheses and to dismiss or selectively ignore information that disconfirms them. Or, as one interviewee nicely put it, you pay more attention or give more weight to things you already believe. That is, the confirmation bias is a form of wishful thinking in which one's desire that a hypothesis be true undermines the objectivity of one's assessment of the evidence that it is. Thus, it can lead one prematurely to stop gathering evidence once the evidence so far gathered confirms what one wants to be true. For example, the confirmation bias operates to maintain false stereotypes about demographic groups.

Though it is natural to want to confirm one's beliefs and counterintuitive to look for evidence that falsifies them, the proper way to overcome the confirmation bias is to look for that evidence.

2.4.2.4   *The Stereotype Bias*

The stereotype bias, an important form of the confirmation bias, is the tendency to over-generalise certain evidence that confirms a belief about a particular category of people. Examples are the gender bias, racial bias, age bias and the blonde stereotype.

2.4.3   Attention Biases

The second group of assessment biases are attention biases, which involve the tendency for one's present concerns to affect one's assessment of evidence.

2.4.3.1   *Tunnel Vision and the Blind Spot Bias*

Tunnel vision is an attention bias that consists in ignoring evidence that goes beyond the scope of one's present concerns. It can cause the blind spot bias, systematically overlooking relevant evidence. In policy matters, tunnel vision can lead advisers to overlook completely a policy's impact on other policies. I illustrate this below with a troubled EU biofuel policy.

2.4.3.2   *The Bias Blind Spot*

Though it does not pertain to the assessment of evidence, the bias blind spot is worth mentioning in the context of the blind spot bias. The term was coined by the social psychologist Emily Pronin and her colleagues Daniel Lin and Lee Ross (Pronin et al. 2002). You suffer from a bias blind spot when you recognize that others' judgments are biased while failing to see that your own are. According to one study conducted in the US, more than 85% of subjects have a bias blind spot in believing that they are less biased than the average American.

2.4.3.3   *The Target Bias*

The target bias, which the biofuel policy also illustrates, involves overly focusing on reaching a proposed goal or target.

2.4.4   Interest-Based Biases

A third group of assessment biases are interest-based biases. These include the self-serving bias and biases toward issues one supports.

2.4.4.1   The Self-Serving Bias

The self-serving bias is the tendency people have to perceive themselves in an overly favourable manner or to seek out and use information selectively in ways that advance or defend their self-interests or justify their behaviour.

2.4.4.2   The Tactical Bias

The tactical bias is the deliberately selective use of evidence to defend one's view. Interest groups and lobbyists often employ this bias when they seek to influence policy on an issue, though it can be used for good, as when simplifying the scientific case for climate change or the health dangers of diesel exhaust. *Merchants of Doubt* (Oreskes and Conway 2010) provides a good example of the tactical bias in the selective evidence that paid climate deniers use to spread doubt and confusion about global warming, exacerbate public fears over the economic consequences of climate action and thereby keep a phoney debate going.

2.4.4.3   The Conflict of Interest Bias

The conflict of interest bias, like the sponsorship bias (Sect. 2.4.1.4), arises when one's financial or other interests compromise the objectivity of one's assessment of evidence. Researchers', advisers' and policy-makers' conflicts of interest undermine professional and public trust in the policy enterprise.

2.4.5   Availability Biases

The next group of assessment biases that I consider are availability biases, which limit the evidence that one has access to, pays attention to or trusts. Availability biases involve the tendency to consider evidence that comes readily to mind or is easily available more representative than it actually is.

2.4.5.1   The Media Bias

In selecting events to report on and stories to publish or broadcast, journalists and news producers tend to pay less attention to what is less striking. Their tendency skews news coverage and limits the availability of information.

This bias is closely related to the reporting bias, which I described above as a research bias.

2.4.5.2 The Anchoring Bias

The anchoring bias consists in the tendency to give too much weight to one piece of evidence (the anchor), e.g., the first piece acquired, the most convincing or the most recent.

2.4.5.3 The Knowledge Bias

The knowledge bias, often called "the curse of knowledge", involves considering only the evidence that one understands or falsely assuming that one's interlocutors have the background knowledge needed to understand the evidence that one presents. When advisers communicate policy options to policy-makers in technical ways, the understanding of which requires a background that policy-makers lack, their knowledge bias affects policy-makers' assessments of those options. Interviewees considered the knowledge bias to be a major challenge for scientific advisers.

2.4.5.4 The Authority Bias

The authority bias consists in accepting what a trusted authority says, even when one lacks the technical background needed to understand it or when the authority speaks about matters outside his or her expertise. For example, in *The Merchants of Doubt* (Oreskes and Conway 2010), Oreskes and Conway explain how 'a handful of scientists obscured the truth on issues from tobacco smoke to global warming'.

2.4.6   Associative Biases

A fifth group of assessment biases are associative biases. An associative bias occurs when associative thinking links otherwise unrelated evidence. For example, emotions can associate evidence in ways that interfere with reflective thinking (thinking slow) and thus activate attention biases (like tunnel vision and blind spots). Association biases that influence one's assessment of evidence are the nature bias, which includes the bio or organic bias; the romantic bias and the ethicality bias (good or evil).

2.4.6.1 The Nature and Bio Biases

In *Principia Ethica* (Moore 1903), the British philosopher G. E. Moore explains the nature bias as an argument that 'a thing is good' because it is 'natural' or bad because it is 'unnatural'. This bias occurs in discussions about gene technologies, food and medicine. The nature bias can be triggered by expressions that one associates with nature, such as the prefix "bio".

2.4.6.2   *The Romantic Bias*
In the romantic bias, the good feelings one experiences when, say, enjoying a wood fire or candles make one resistant to the evidence that wood fires contribute to particulate air pollution (Reeve et al. 2013; Semmens et al. 2015) or that candle smoke is carcinogenic (Skovmand et al. 2017). Appeals to tradition can involve the romantic bias (and the nature bias).

2.4.6.3   *The Ethicality Bias*
The ethicality bias is the tendency to abide by an initial association of evidence with good or evil. Kahneman argues that the brain responds quickly to emotionally loaded words, and associating new evidence with good or evil can undermine rational thinking about it.

2.5   ILLUSTRATIONS

In this section, I describe three real and very consequential cases of how new evidence, various biases and the desire to eliminate cognitive dissonance jointly contributed to irrational decision-making. I summarize each case, describe interviewees' responses to it and identify the biases and cognitive dissonance it illustrates.

2.5.1   *Gilles-Éric Séralini on Roundup and GM*
The first case study is the so-called "Séralini affair".

2.5.1.1   *The Séralini Affair in a Nutshell*
The Séralini affair centred on the French molecular biologist Gilles-Éric Séralini's article 'Long-Term Toxicity of a Roundup Herbicide and a Roundup-Tolerant Genetically Modified Maize' (Séralini et al. 2012a). First published in September 2012 in the Elsevier publishing group's peer-reviewed journal *Food and Chemical Toxicology*, the article reported an increase in the number of tumours in rats fed Monsanto's genetically modified corn and its herbicide RoundUp. Shortly after its publication, the

journal's editor received letters expressing doubts about the validity of the findings, criticism of the study's animal models and allegations of fraud.

The paper was widely discussed in the media. Debora MacKenzie summarized the criticisms in 'Study Linking GM Crops and Cancer Questioned' published in *New Scientist* (MacKenzie 2012). According to MacKenzie, Séralini had used too few rats to obtain reliable data. And since he used the Sprague Dawly strain of laboratory rat, which is known to develop tumours at a high rate, the incidence of tumours he reported could have been normal. Finally, his statistical analyses and interpretation of data were unconventional and complicated, and his toxicological methods were not reliable.

Elsevier announced on November 28, 2013, that *Food and Chemical Toxicology* had retracted the article (Séralini et al. 2012b). However, in June 2014 *Environmental Sciences Europe* republished it with the complete data set in response to requests from national regulatory bodies (Séralini et al. 2014). The journal's editor commented that the paper had not undergone another peer review 'because this had already been conducted by *Food and Chemical Toxicology*, who had concluded there had been no fraud nor misrepresentation.' Republication renewed the controversy and added discussion of the behaviour of both journals' editors to it.

2.5.1.2   *Interviewees' Reflections on the Controversy*

I asked interviewees about when they read an article with an open mind and when they believe that it is not reliable. The following two situations illustrate their reflections.

Imagine you are an anti-GM or anti-Monsanto activist. You see a paper entitled 'Long-Term Toxicity of a Roundup Herbicide and a Roundup-Tolerant Genetically Modified Maize', which is music to your ears. You go straight to the conclusions, skipping everything else. You then tell your activist colleagues about these new findings proving that GM crops are carcinogenic.

Imagine that you are a scientist working on the safety of GM crops and years of research have convinced you that they are safe for human consumption. Seeing the eye-catchingly titled paper, you delve into its sections on methodology and statistics and realize that the study was flawed.

2.5.1.3   *Biases and Cognitive Dissonance in the Séralini Case*

The case illustrates many biases. In Séralini's collection of evidence, one can see the sampling and reporting biases. The confirmation and tactical biases were at work in his interpretation of the evidence. According to interviewees, readers were affected by their confirmation biases, depending of their background, and the authority bias, since Séralini's paper was first published in a peer reviewed journal. So, in the Séralini case people were affected by different biases and by the same biases to different degrees.

One's reaction to the paper would depend on one's view. The anti-GM or anti-Monsanto activist, who was glad about the paper's publication, might accept the evidence, because of the confirmation bias, without double-checking it, as opposed to the GM researcher, who reacted to the paper by explaining why its research was not reliable. That scientist might experience cognitive dissonance when first viewing the paper, for he or she believes that its claims are false, but, since they appear in a peer-reviewed journal, the authority bias leads him or her to believe that they may be justified. Hoping to find evidence that the research is unreliable, he or she goes to the sections on methodology and statistical analysis. There the scientist finds what he or she wanted, thereby relieving the dissonance.

2.5.2   Andrew Wakefield on the MMR Vaccine

2.5.2.1   Wakefield's Lancet Paper
The "Wakefield-MMR vaccine case" began with the publication of Andrew Wakefield's paper 'Autism, Inflammatory Bowel Disease, and MMR Vaccine' in *The Lancet* in February 1998 (Wakefield et al. 1998), in which he claimed to have found a statistically significant link between the combined measles, mumps and rubella (MMR) vaccine and autism spectrum disorders. An investigation by the journalist Brian Deer (2009) found that Wakefield had manipulated his data and failed to disclose multiple conflicts of interest, among other ethical violations. *The Lancet* partially retracted the paper in 2004 (Horton 2004), its editor-in-chief Richard Horton saying he did not have the evidence to do more before the General Medical Council (GMC) had completed its investigation. In May 2010, the GMC found Wakefield guilty of serious professional misconduct, and he was removed from the Medical Register, meaning he could no longer practise medicine in the UK. Horton then fully retracted the paper, stating, 'It was utterly clear, without any ambiguity at all, that the statements in the paper were utterly false'. After receiving further information on Wakefield's research practices from Deer, *The BMJ* published a signed editorial in 2011 that said Wakefield's paper was fraudulent (Deer 2011).

But Wakefield's claims had already been widely reported (Goldacre 2009), leading to a sharp drop in vaccination rates in the UK and Ireland and increases in the incidences of measles and mumps, with some cases resulting in death or permanent impairment (McIntyre and Leask 2008; Pepys 2007). Following the paper's publication, several large epidemiological studies were undertaken, and reviews of the evidence by the US Center for Disease Control and Prevention, the American Academy of Paediatrics, the Institute of Medicine of the US National Academy of Sciences (NAS 2004), the UK National Health Service (NHS 2012) and the Cochrane Library (Demicheli et al. 2013) all concluded that there was no link between the MMR vaccine and autism. However, the new research did not relieve the public's fear of vaccination.

The damage was done. Worse, it was done by a medical doctor. Wakefield's paper was described as 'perhaps, the most damaging medical hoax of the last 100 years' (Flaherty 2011). Physicians, medical researchers and the editors of medical journals (Deer 2011; Godlee 2011) blamed Wakefield for epidemics and deaths.

2.5.2.2   How Could a Fraudulent Paper Have Had Such an Effect on Vaccination Rates?

Interviewees were aware that the decrease in vaccinations has led to outbreaks of diseases, such as measles, that had almost been eliminated and blamed social media for having spread doubts. It seemed to them that lay people have more influence than scientific authorities. They were worried about anti-vaccination campaigns and puzzled by their success.

It seems that many people do not understand how vaccines work, and the continuing stream of contradictory arguments confuses them. In 'Of Natural Bodies and Antibodies: Parents' Vaccine Refusal and the Dichotomies of Natural and Artificial' (Reich 2016), Jennifer A. Reich analyses why parents are increasingly rejecting vaccines for their children. She argues that they construct a dichotomy between the natural and the artificial according to which vaccines, as artificial interventions, are unnecessary, ineffective and potentially dangerous. This is the nature bias. Thus, I believe that the nature bias is to a certain extent responsible for the success of the anti-vaccine movement.

2.5.2.3   Biases and Cognitive Dissonance in the Wakefield Case

The case 'Wakefield-MMR vaccine' illustrates experimenter biases (in collecting evidence), the conflict of interest bias and the authority bias (in that a medical doctor authored the paper). Those who reject vaccination clearly evidence the confirmation bias. Researchers and policy-makers are guilty of the knowledge bias *vis-à-vis* the public. Perhaps most significantly, Reich's study reveals the effects of the nature bias.

2.5.3   The European Biofuel Policy

The third case involves a European biofuel policy, European Directive 2003/30/EC (Directive 2003), promoting the use of biofuels in transportation.

2.5.3.1   A Policy Intended to Address Climate Change

Plant-based biofuels are alternatives to fossil fuels. As Didier Bourguignon explains, first-generation or conventional biofuels are made from starch, sugar and oil derived from harvested plants or the residues of harvest, such as straw. They are renewable energy sources (Bourguignon 2015). In the early 2000s, there was a lot of interest in biofuels, which were thought to emit less CO_2 than fossil fuels, as part of the transition to a low-carbon economy. However, their lower CO_2 emission was later questioned.

Bourguignon compiled a concise overview of the EU's policy for subsidizing biofuel production as part of European Directive 2003/30/EC (Bourguignon 2015, 2017). The policy was initially a measure for lowering CO_2 emission in the transportation sector in order to meet the targets set in the Kyoto Protocol. However, promoting the use of biofuels had unintended consequences that adversely affected other policies. For one, it classified biomass, and so wood, as a renewable source of energy. However, burning wood emits significant amounts of particulate pollution, which has a considerable impact on health. For another, critics criticised the policy for indirectly inducing changes in land use that triggered an increase in global food prices, causing food insecurity for the poor.

In 2008, the Food and Agriculture Organization (FAO), which leads the United Nations' international efforts to eliminate hunger, sounded the alarm over the policy. In their report 'Biofuels: Prospects, Risks and Opportunities' (Food and Agriculture Organization 2008), the FAO confirmed that the demand for biofuels, which was rapidly growing as a result of the policy, was contributing to higher food prices and threatening the food security of both urban and rural poor net food buyers, especially in developing countries. In the same year, the Scientific Committee of the European Environment Agency (EEA) published its opinion on the environmental impact of the European public's use of biofuels (EEA 2008). The committee recommended a comprehensive study on the environmental risks and benefits of biofuels.

European Directive 2003/30/EC was enacted as part of meeting the EU's climate change commitment, which called for a 20% cut in greenhouse gas emissions from 1990 levels, 20% of EU energy coming from renewable sources and a 20% improvement in energy efficiency, all by 2020. But the policy was enacted without considering the full range of its effects.

So, what happened with the biofuel policy? EU policy-makers acknowledged its adverse effects, and the EU revised it. According to Bourguignon (2015, 2017), the EU shifted its support from conventional biofuels to advanced second-generation biofuels in 2015. As these are made from various types of non-food-crop biomass, they do not compete with food crops.

2.5.3.2   Reflections on How the Policy's Adverse Effects May Have Been Overlooked

Interviewees found this case very striking, and some brought it up spontaneously as an example of an issue about which the evidence made them change their mind. With the advantage of hindsight, they said that advisers should have included a wider range of evidence in their assessment of the promise of first-generation biofuels and investigated a wider range of possible side effects with an open mind.

2.5.3.3   Biases and Cognitive Dissonance in the Biofuel Case

Several biases are easy to see in the EU biofuel policy case:

- tunnel vision in that excessive focus on the 20% targets created a blind spot hiding the consequences of stimulating the production of biofuel and obscuring the policy's real aim, which was to mitigate climate change;
- the target bias in overly focusing on the goals of 20% of energy from renewable resources;
- the bio bias may have made *bio*fuel seem good.

2.6   THE BIAS WHEEL: A TOOL FOR BIAS-AWARENESS IN SCIENTIFIC ADVISING

To conclude this chapter, I summarise the biases that are most relevant in the science-policy ecosystem in the bias wheel in Fig. 2.1. The bias wheel is a tool to enhance its users' critical thinking by making them aware of their biases. Its ultimate aim is to enable advisers to overcome their biases, or at least some of them, in judging evidence. For I claim that bias-awareness reduces one's biases toward new information so that one considers it with

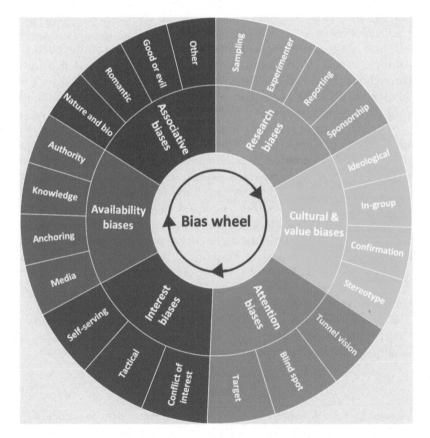

Fig. 2.1   The bias wheel: a tool for becoming aware of biases in scientific advising

a more open mind than one otherwise would. This, in turn, can make evidence-based policy decisions more robust.

2.7   Chapter Summary and Conclusions

"We all see only that which we are trained to see"
Robert Anton Wilson in 'Masks of the Illuminati', 1981

Scientific advisers should be as unbiased as possible in formulating for policy-makers all of the policy options that the scientific and societal evidence supports.

A bias is a mental inclination or disposition in a certain direction. It obstructs critical thinking and, as a result, the rationality of decisions. Throughout the scientific advisory process, biases can cause advisers to fail to weigh evidence, assessments and points of view objectively. In other words, bias distorts assessment.

I introduced three real and consequential cases in this chapter and will refer to them in later chapters. The first involved Séralini's claims about the toxicity of the herbicide RoundUp and GM maize. Séralini's study was first published in a peer-reviewed journal; it was then retracted after its results were shown to be unreliable and it was republished in another peer-reviewed journal, though without a new review. Scientists believe that the case undermined the public's trust in science. The second case involved Wakefield's claim to have found a correlation between the MMR vaccine and autism spectrum disorders. Wakefield had manipulated evidence and failed to declare multiple conflicts of interest, and the study was declared to be fraudulent. The third case was the EU's decision to subsidise biofuels, which had unintended consequences for land use and food prices.

The bias wheel synthesises the described biases and is a tool to make advisers aware of their biases and, ultimately, overcome some of them in judging evidence and policy options.

References

Aronson, E., T. D. Wilson, R. M. Akert, and S. Sommers. 2018. *Social Psychology*. 9th ed., Global ed. New York: Pearson.
Bourguignon, D. 2015. *EU Biofuels Policy Dealing with Indirect Land Use Change*. Brussels: European Parliamentary Research Service.

Bourguignon, D. 2017. *Advanced Biofuels: Technologies and EU Policy*. Brussels: European Parliamentary Research Service.

Bowls. n.d. Lawn Bowling—A Complete Beginners' Guide. Retrieved from https://www.bowls.org.uk/flat-green. Accessed November 11, 2018.

Compernolle, T. 2014. *BrainChains: Discover Your Brain and Unleash Its Full Potential in a Hyperconnected Multitasking World*. London: Compublications.

Cross, R. 1998. "The Trajectory of a Ball in Lawn Bowls." *American Journal of Physics* 66 (8): 735–738. https://doi.org/10.1119/1.19028.

Deer, B. 2009. MMR Doctor Andrew Wakefield Fixed Data on Autism. *The Times*. Retrieved from https://www.thetimes.co.uk/article/mmr-doctor-andrew-wakefield-fixed-data-on-autism-mgj82qsk50g.

Deer, B. 2011. "How the Vaccine Crisis Was Meant to Make Money." *British Medical Journal* 342 (7789). https://doi.org/10.1136/bmj.c5258.

Demicheli, V., A. Rivetti, M. G. Debalini, and C. Di Pietrantonj. 2013. "Vaccines for Measles, Mumps and Rubella in Children." *Evidence-Based Child Health: A Cochrane Review Journal* 8 (6): 2076–2238. https://doi.org/10.1002/ebch.1948.

Directive 2003/30/EC of the European Parliament and of the Council of 8 May 2003 on the Promotion of the Use of Biofuels or Other Renewable Fuels for Transport L 123 C.F.R. (2003).

European Environment Agency (EEA). 2008. *Suspend 10 Percent Biofuels Target, Says EEA's Scientific Advisory Body*. 30 April 2008 ed. Copenhagen: European Environment Agency.

Festinger, L. 1957. *A Theory of Cognitive Dissonance*. Evanston, IL: Row, Peterson.

Flaherty, D. K. 2011. "The Vaccine-Autism Connection: A Public Health Crisis Caused by Unethical Medical Practices and Fraudulent Science." *Annals of Pharmacotherapy* 45 (10): 1302–1304. https://doi.org/10.1345/aph.1q318.

Food and Agriculture Organization (FAO). 2008. *The State of Food and Agriculture 2008. Biofuels: Prospects, Risks and Opportunities*.

Godlee, F. 2011. "The Fraud Behind the MMR Scare." *British Medical Journal* 342 (January 6). https://doi.org/10.1136/bmj.d22.

Goldacre, B. 2009. *Bad Science*. Paperback ed. London: Fourth Estate.

Goldstein, E. B. 2011. *Cognitive Psychology*. 3rd ed. Australia, Belmont, CA: Wadsworth/Cengage Learning.

Horton, R. 2004. "A Statement by the Editors of The Lancet." *The Lancet* 363 (9411): 820–821. https://doi.org/10.1016/s0140-6736(04)15699-7.

Huff, D. 1954. *How to Lie with Statistics*. New York: Norton.

Kahneman, D. 2012. *Thinking, Fast and Slow*. London: Penguin Books.

Keville, T. D. 1994. "The Invisible Woman: Gender Bias in Medical Research." *Women's Rights Law Reporter* 15: 123–142.

Krimsky, S. 2013. "Do Financial Conflicts of Interest Bias Research? An Inquiry into the 'Funding Effect' Hypothesis." *Science, Technology, & Human Values* 38 (4): 566–587. https://doi.org/10.1177/0162243912456271.

MacKenzie, D. 2012. "Study Linking GM Crops and Cancer Questioned." *New Scientist*. Retrieved from https://www.newscientist.com/article/dn22287-study-linking-gm-crops-and-cancer-questioned/.

McIntyre, P., and J. Leask. 2008. "Improving Uptake of MMR Vaccine." *British Medical Journal* 336 (7647): 729. https://doi.org/10.1136/bmj.39503. 508484.80.

Mercier, H., and D. Sperber. 2017. *The Enigma of Reason: A New Theory of Human Understanding*. London: Allen Lane.

Moore, G. E. 1903. *Principia Ethica*. Cambridge: Cambridge University Press.

NAS. 2004. *Immunization Safety Review: Vaccines and Autism*. Edited by N. A. O. Sciences. Washington, DC: National Academy of Sciences.

NHS. 2012. *MMR the Facts*. Edited by In D. O. H. P. NHS Immunisation Information. London, UK: National archives.gov.uk.

Oreskes, N., and E. M. Conway. 2010. *Merchants of Doubt: How a Handful of Scientists Obscured the Truth on Issues from Tobacco Smoke to Global Warming*. 1st U.S. ed. New York and London: Bloomsbury Press.

Pepys, M. B. 2007. "Science and Serendipity." *Clinical Medicine (London, England)* 7(6): 562. https://doi.org/10.3399/096016407782604776.

Pielke, R. A. 2007. *The Honest Broker: Making Sense of Science in Policy and Politics*. Cambridge: Cambridge University Press.

Pronin, E., D. Y. Lin, and L. Ross. 2002. "The Bias Blind Spot: Perceptions of Bias in Self Versus Others." *Personality and Social Psychology Bulletin* 28 (3): 369–381. https://doi.org/10.1177/0146167202286008.

Reeve, I., J. Scott, D. Hine, and N. Bhullar. 2013. "'This Is Not a Burning Issue for Me': How Citizens Justify Their Use of Wood Heaters in a City with a Severe Air Pollution Problem." *Energy Policy* 57: 204.

Reich, J. A. 2016. "Of Natural Bodies and Antibodies: Parents' Vaccine Refusal and the Dichotomies of Natural and Artificial." *Social Science & Medicine* 157 (C): 103–110. https://doi.org/10.1016/j.socscimed.2016.04.001.

Semmens, E. O., C. W. Noonan, R. W. Allen, E. C. Weiler, and T. J. Ward. 2015. "Indoor Particulate Matter in Rural, Wood Stove Heated Homes." *Environmental Research* 138: 93–100. https://doi.org/10.1016/j.envres.2015.02.005.

Séralini, G.-E., E. Clair, R. Mesnage, S. Gress, N. Defarge, M. Malatesta, D. Hennequin, and J. S. de Vendômois. 2012a. "Long Term Toxicity of a Roundup Herbicide and a Roundup-Tolerant Genetically Modified Maize." *Food and Chemical Toxicology: An International Journal Published for the British Industrial Biological Research Association* 50 (11): 4221. https://doi.org/10.1016/j.fct.2012.08.005.

Séralini, G.-E., E. Clair, R. Mesnage, S. Gress, N. Defarge, M. Malatesta, D. Hennequin, and J. S. de Vendômois. 2012b. "RETRACTED: Long Term Toxicity of a Roundup Herbicide and a Roundup-Tolerant Genetically Modified Maize." *Food and Chemical Toxicology* 50 (11): 4221–4231. https://doi.org/10.1016/j.fct.2012.08.005.

Séralini, G.-E., E. Clair, R. Mesnage, S. Gress, N. Defarge, M. Malatesta, D. Hennequin, and J. S. de Vendômois. 2014. "Republished Study: Long-Term Toxicity of a Roundup Herbicide and a Roundup-Tolerant Genetically Modified Maize." *Environmental Sciences Europe* 26 (1): 14. https://doi.org/10.1186/s12302-014-0014-5.

Šimundić, A.-M. 2013. "Bias in Research." *Biochemia Medica* 23 (1): 12–15. https://doi.org/10.11613/bm.2013.003.

Skovmand, A., A. C. Damiao Gouveia, I. K. Koponen, P. Møller, S. Loft, and M. Roursgaard. 2017. "Lung Inflammation and Genotoxicity in Mice Lungs After Pulmonary Exposure to Candle Light Combustion Particles." *Toxicology Letters* 276: 31–38. https://doi.org/10.1016/j.toxlet.2017.04.015.

Spencer, H. 1873. *The Study of Sociology*. London: Henry S. King. Consulted on http://oll.libertyfund.org/titles/spencer-the-study-of-sociology-1873.

Spiegelhalter, D. 2017. "Trust in Numbers." *Journal of the Royal Statistical Society: Series A (Statistics in Society)* 180 (4): 948–965. https://doi.org/10.1111/rssa.12302.

Tholen, B. 2017. *Virtue and Responsibility in Policy Research and Advice*. New York, NY: Springer.

Turner, M. E., and A. R. Pratkanis. 1998. "Twenty-Five Years of Groupthink Theory and Research: Lessons from the Evaluation of a Theory." *Organizational Behavior and Human Decision Processes* 73 (2–3): 105–115. https://doi.org/10.1006/obhd.1998.2756.

Wakefield, A. J., S. H. Murch, A. Anthony, et al. 1998. "Ileal–Lymphoid–Nodular Hyperplasia, Non-specific Colitis, and Pervasive Developmental Disorder in Children." *Lancet* 351: 637–641.

Wikisource Contributors. 2019. "1911 Encyclopædia Britannica/Bowls." *Wikisource*. https://en.wikisource.org/w/index.php?title=1911_Encyclop%C3%A6dia_Britannica/Bowls&oldid=5459858. Accessed June 25, 2019.

CHAPTER 3

Scientific Foresight: Considering the Future of Science and Technology

Abstract This chapter focuses on the societal elements that complement scientific evidence. It explains how foresight methods give advisers insights into how scientific and technological developments may impact society, often unintendedly and offers a detailed scheme, STEEPED, for investigating all such foreseeable impacts from the widest range, 360 degrees, of perspectives. It also describes the use of future scenarios in exploring possible future impacts of today's developments.

Keywords Scientific foresight · Foresight methods · Societal context · STEEPED · Scenario-based foresight · Unintended impacts

> Foresight is not about predicting the future, it's about minimizing surprise.
> —Karl Schroeder (2011)

Foresight is a methodology for systematically thinking about the future by envisioning a wide range of possible futures, from likely to very unlikely and from desirable to undesirable, and mapping paths likely to lead to, or away from, them. So, foresight exercises are designed to enable advisers and policy-makers to steer towards a desirable future and respond proactively to it by crafting policies to meet its challenges. Advisers' foresight studies complement the scientific evidence with evidence of the possible societal

© The Author(s) 2020
L. Van Woensel, *A Bias Radar for Responsible Policy-Making*,
St Antony's Series, https://doi.org/10.1007/978-3-030-32126-0_3

consequences of the tentative policy alternatives they investigate. Advisers translate these possible futures into the policy options that constitute their advice to policy-makers. So, the power of scientific foresight is that it enhances policy-makers' ability to anticipate the possible future impacts of their policy decisions on society and plan for them before they arise.

In this chapter, I first give an overview of the most common foresight methods. I then explain the difference between scientific and technological foresight, on the one hand, and technology assessment, on the other. Next, I explain some of the different kinds of societal impacts advisers can consider in their foresight investigations. This is followed by my presentation of a method, STEEPED, for investigating technological developments and their possible impacts on society from 360 degrees of perspectives. I next describe how to set up foresight conversations with groups of stakeholders' representatives. Finally, I explain the benefits of including a variety of stakeholders in foresight conversations. I illustrate the chapter's themes with the European Parliament's foresight study of robotics and artificial intelligence.

3.1   Foresight Methods

Foresight practitioners can choose from a range of methods, depending on the reason for their foresight study and their resources. But it is not among the aims of this book to compare foresight methodologies, and I consider only scenario-based foresight. However, in this section I give a brief overview of some of the most common foresight methods and terminology. Additional readings are listed in Appendix B.

The purpose of advisers' foresight studies is to enable policy-makers to anticipate and respond proactively to a policy's possible future complications. Therefore, they should always be a part of the determination of policy. Some readers may be uncomfortable about including foresight in the advisory process because, while the uncertainties that the scientific evidence reveals are largely quantifiable, foresight investigations generate qualitative and even value-laden considerations.

The two most relevant publications on policy-oriented foresight methods are Angela Wilkinson's *Strategic Foresight Primer* (Wilkinson 2017) and the UK's *Futures Toolkit* (Government Office for Science [UK] 2017), published by one of the EU's first governmental foresight institutes. Also very useful for foresight practitioners is *Foresight: A Glossary* (Centre for Strategic Futures 2017) and Maree Conway's *Creating and Sustaining*

Social Foresight in Australia: A Review of Government Foresight (Conway and Stewart **2005**).

3.1.1 Horizon Scanning

Scientific foresight (Sect. 3.2) always starts with horizon scanning, which is systematically investigating present trends among events and their foreseeable developments to predict and anticipate potential threats and opportunities, especially with regard to emerging technology and its effects on society. In a scientific foresight study, horizon scanning is usually a traditional technology-assessment study covering the state of the art and what is emerging. So, I call it a "technical horizon scan". Technical horizon scans include advisers' assessments of how the evidence pertaining to the technology's future relates to the problem that they are investigating. At the European Parliament, STOA's[1] technical horizon scans include preliminary assessments of a technology's possible societal impacts from a wide range of perspectives in accordance with the STEEPED scheme explained below.

3.1.2 Delphi

Developed by the Rand Corporation in the 1970s, the Delphi foresight method is, according to the Government Office for Science (UK) (2017), a 'consultation process used to gather opinion from a wide group of subject experts about the future and to prioritise the issues of strategic importance.' A Delphi is usually run in two or more rounds, in each of which the experts in the group answer a questionnaire. After each round, a facilitator generates an anonymised summary of their answers and their reasons for them. In the next round, they are encouraged to revise their earlier answers in the light of the other participants' earlier answers. In this way, the method generates consensus. The Delphi method is based on the principle that a group's judgement is more accurate than that of a random collection of individuals. Nowadays, there are also web-based Delphis, in which experts see each others' answers on-line in real time. On-line Delphis are more interactive and faster.

---

[1] Studies conducted for the Panel of the Future of Science and Technology (STOA).

3.1.3   Visioning and Envisioning

In visioning, experts generate a consensus description of a most preferred future state and usually also a consensus backcasting or roadmap of specific actions for progressing towards that state.

Scientific policy advisers' foresight investigations employ envisioning, in which advisers, stakeholders and invited experts describe a variety of possible future states without seeking consensus on their relative desirability, and advisers generate backcastings for each.

In both methods, one scans for both individual and group values, but in envisioning one also scans for participants' concerns, hopes and fears without judging them. Envisioning brings a divergent range of alternative possible futures into consideration, while the results of visioning converge on the ones that the experts want.

3.1.4   Scenario-Based Foresight

Scenario-based foresight is a method of strategic decision-making; it is the foresight method I recommend for scientific policy advising. Scenarios are mere descriptions, not predictions or forecasts, of possible futures. More precisely, they are imaginary descriptions. Advisers use them to explore possible futures in a foresight conversation, and policy-makers can use them to think more concretely about uncertain aspects of the future. Because scenario-based foresight employs all kinds of scenarios, it considers probable and unlikely and desirable and undesirable futures. So, it alerts policy-makers to what could happen and in this way can even prevent crises (see Sect. 3.3).

3.1.5   Cross-Impact Analysis

Cross-impact analysis is a method of anticipating how present trends may evolve and thus of reducing uncertainty about the future. In policy work, it can be used as a sort of stress test to help policy-makers evaluate the adequacy of present policies by identifying their unintended problematic consequences (see Chapter 4).

3.1.6   More Foresight Terms

To provide more background, I explain some of the other foresight terms in *Foresight: A Glossary* (Centre for Strategic Futures 2017).

- **Black swans and wildcards**. A black swan is an impactful event beyond the realm of normal expectations. According to Nassim Taleb (2010), black swans, like 9/11 and the invention of the Internet, illustrate the inadequacy of human estimates of the future and purely empirical methods of anticipating it. Black swans are extreme cases of wildcards, which are low-probability, high-impact future events whose occurrences would be immensely disruptive but for which there is no present evidence, e.g., a global Internet breakdown.
- **Driving forces**. Driving forces are observable significant trends that are expected to continue, e.g., artificial intelligence and the ageing of society. The social impact of some driving forces, like artificial intelligence, are uncertain.
- **Emerging issues**. An emerging issue is a new technology, policy question, etc. that may become a critical mainstream trend or issue.
- **Forecast**. Forecasts are predictions of future events or trends on the basis of past and present trends.
- **Strategic foresight**. Strategic foresight is the employment of scenarios and backcastings to choose the course of action that leads to the future one wants.
- **Systems thinking**. Systems thinking is a holistic analytical approach to problems that considers the full range of a system's components and their interactions (see Chapters 1 and 5).
- **Trends analysis**. Trends analysis is a method of identifying patterns in events. So, one can also use it to identify events to prepare for. Technological trends analysis and the analysis of emerging trends are important in scientific foresight work. For example, the report 'How Blockchain Technology Could Change Our Lives' (Boucher 2017) supported a series of activities on blockchain at the European Parliament.
- **Wicked problems**. A wicked problem is one with no simple solution because its nature resists precise characterization. Wicked problems commonly arise in complex environments with constantly evolving interdependencies, e.g., climate change.

- **Wind-tunnelling**. Wind-tunnelling is a method of assessing the robustness of backcastings to possible futures.

3.2   Scientific Foresight

Scientific policy advising employs scientific foresight to take it beyond assessing the scientific evidence pertaining to a technology by including the results of envisioning the technology's possible societal impacts. After explaining technology assessment, I describe the aims of scientific foresight interventions and using them to prepare for desirable and undesirable futures.

3.2.1   Technology Assessment

Technology assessment has a much longer tradition than does scientific foresight. It originally consisted in providing policy-makers with policy alternatives for solving problems in the development and use of technology.

In *What Is Technology Assessment?* (Banta 2009), David Banta describes technology as scientific knowledge applied to a definite practical purpose, and he characterizes technology assessment as a form of policy research that tries to predict the short and long-term consequences of applications of technologies. *Bridges Between Science, Society and Policy*, which summarizes the results of the two-year project 'Technology Assessment in Europe: Between Method and Impact' (TAMI), (Decker and Ladikas 2004), which brought together the main parliamentary and non-parliamentary European institutes of technology assessment, describes technology assessment as:

> …problem oriented research which aims to contribute to solutions of political, social, ecological, etc. problems, i.e., problems deriving from outside the realm of science and technology. The results of TA are, in general, concrete recommendations to policy-makers and therefore the original questioning as well as the area of potential impact is outside the scientific system.

Focusing on its contributions to solving social problems, TAMI's participants proposed the following definition of TA:

Technology assessment (TA) is a scientific, interactive and communicative process which aims to contribute to the formation of public and political opinion on societal aspects of science and technology.

According to this definition, TA (1) provides knowledge, (2) involves societal interactions with stakeholders and (3) includes communication that contributes to the formation of public and political opinion.

3.2.2   *The Aims of Scientific Foresight*

Scientific foresight is a method of conducting TA in a time frame of 10 years or more in the future that incorporates a systematized approach to a technology's societal effects. Scientific or technological foresight, which I use interchangeably, consists in participating, in one way or another, with members of society to learn about the future of scientific and technological developments, especially complicated technologies whose applications raise many uncertainties for society. According to Kees van der Heijden in *Scenarios: The Art of Strategic Conversation* (Van der Heijden 2005), its aims include:

1. Addressing a specific problem or question, e.g., how we can organise waste management to achieve a circular economy within 20 years;
2. Making sense of a puzzling situation, e.g., whether we should be wary of artificial intelligence;
3. Planning for action, e.g., by identifying trends that we should prepare for.

The Handbook of Technology Foresight (Georghiou et al. 2009) adds:

- Extending the breadth of knowledge and vision of the future;
- Bringing new actors into strategic debates;
- Informing policy and public debates in areas where science and innovation play a significant role;
- Improving policy implementation by enabling informed 'buy-in' to decision-making processes.

The *Handbook* authors also describe foresight as a participative methodology that extends the breadth of knowledge and the depth of analyses available to decision-makers. Finally, the authors of *Foresight in Action* (van Asselt et al. 2010) describe 'policy-oriented foresight' as assessments of the future in the context of public policy.

A scientific foresight intervention adds a normative dimension to a traditional technology assessment by studying how citizens and other stakeholders envision the possible impacts of a technology's anticipated applications and of policies for it. And unlike a technology forecast, a foresight intervention investigates possible futures to, for instance, anticipate citizens' concerns about an emerging technology and formulate guidelines for its use. Policy-makers use the policy options that foresight investigators envision and assess to craft policies that will likely lead to desirable futures.

3.2.3   Unintended and Perverse Impacts

In scientific foresight, unintended impacts are the consequences of a scientific or technological development or a policy that developers or policy-makers had not foreseen. An example I have already mentioned is the competition between fuel and food crops that followed upon the EU's promotion of biofuels. New developments and policies can also have perverse impacts, which offset their intended consequences. For instance, more fuel-efficient cars were developed in order to save energy, but they have also made driving cheaper, and the resulting tendency toward increased driving offsets their intended effect. Similarly, low-tar cigarettes were meant to improve public health, but they have led some smokers to smoke more.

3.2.4   Hard and Soft Impacts

A scientific foresight study of a new scientific or technological development investigates both practical risks, on which the developers of technology and policy-makers tend to focus, and social and ethical risks, which typically concern philosophers of technology and the public (Swierstra and te Molder 2012).

New technologies promise us better health, cleaner air and more free time. But they also explode, poison and pollute. These unintended consequences are hard impacts, i.e., they can be easily identified and measured. As Tsjalling Swierstra and Hedwig te Molder explain, typical hard impacts are risks and harms to safety, health and the environment. Hard impacts demand policies and regulations that lessen them.

But technologies do much more than perform their functions; they also shape how we live, how we experience the world and what we value. Think of smartphones. They push us to rethink certain norms: how we use them politely in the presence of others and how we respond to the pull to check them constantly and the pressure of always being reachable. Such soft impacts are not easy to identify; they are not quantifiable; there is no consensus that they are harmful and it is not always clear who, if anyone, is to blame for them. A technology does not directly cause its soft impacts, for they consist in how we use it. Other soft impacts are the fears that we forget how to drive as a result of using self-driving cars, lose our general knowledge because of the Internet and feel that we must have perfect teeth because of orthodontic technology. And devices intended to save us time could speed society up and increase time scarcity.

Because soft impacts are qualitative and the values they affect are unclear or contested, technologists largely ignore them, and policy-makers dismiss them as too fuzzy to take seriously in determining public policy, at best acknowledging that they are private concerns. However, Tsjalling Swierstra, who was involved in the European Parliament's first scientific foresight study (STOA 2016), argues that we can no longer afford to ignore technology's soft impacts because they are increasingly prominent in prosperous societies, where technologies become more and more 'intimate' as they further pervade our lives (Swierstra 2015). According to Swierstra, anticipating soft impacts and their distinct normative challenges requires detailed descriptions of the plausible techno-moral changes emerging technologies will bring. But getting soft impacts onto the agenda of policy-makers and technologists is not a simple matter (Swierstra and te Molder 2012).

3.3   Assessing Future Impacts

I advocate scenario-based foresight in preparing future-oriented scientific policy advice, for scenarios are a good way to envision how scientific and technological developments might impact the future.

3.3.1   Scenarios for Exploring Future Uncertainties

Scenarios are stories about the future; their purpose is to inform better decisions in the present.

First used by the Shell Oil Company, scenarios are fictional stories that articulate risks and opportunities in a range of imaginable futures. Scientific foresight practitioners use them to stimulate discussion about how to plan for the long term and shape the real future (Centre for Strategic Futures 2017; Kahane 2012; Schwartz 1998). That is why scientific policy advisers should practice scenario-based foresight.

Shell, which has used scenarios since the early 1970s (Wilkinson and Kupers 2014), shared its experience in *Scenarios: An Explorer's Guide* (Shell International Ltd. 2008), in which the company explains:

> ...decision makers can use scenarios to think about the uncertain aspects of the future that most worry them, and to explore the ways in which these might unfold. Such scenarios should address the same important questions and all include those aspects of the future that are likely to persist (that is, the predetermined elements), but each one describes a different way in which the uncertain aspects of the future could play out.

So, scenarios allow us to develop a shared understanding of how the context in which we operate may evolve. In *The Art of the Long View* (Schwartz 1998), Peter Schwartz describes scenarios as a tool for ordering one's thoughts about alternative future environments in which one's decisions might play out, and that is how we scientific foresight practitioners use them. I call them "explorative scenarios".

Explorative scenarios are the basis for strategic conversations with groups of stakeholders about the potential effects of scientific and technological developments on them and their possible responses. So, they are a shared basis for exploring future uncertainties and making rational decisions (Shell International Ltd. 2008).

3.3.2   The Desirability of Futures

Individual stakeholders prefer some futures to others, but their preferences differ. Vegetarians and those worried about climate change may want a future in which we do not eat meat, but those who enjoy meat or earn their living producing it will not want that future. Scientific advisers must incorporate stakeholders' preferences into their advice, but because they must be impartial, they may not include their personal views about the desirability of those futures, which is for policy-makers to decide. Advisers figure out policy paths for reaching certain futures and avoiding others.

3.3.3   Scenarios from Diverse Perspectives

Advisers should develop explorative scenarios from a variety of perspectives, for this enables them to look at a scientific or technological development with open minds. The Shell Company's book (Shell International Ltd. 2008) compares writing an explorative scenario with drawing a map of the world. As the world map projections with the North Pole and the South Pole in the centre (Figs. 3.1 and 3.2) illustrate, there are many perspectives from which to map the world, and putting the North Pole in the centre rather than at the top may lead to new insights, for example, about transportation, tourism or national defence, or get us to re-examine our assumptions about the consequences of melting polar ice as a result of developing the Arctic.

Similarly, in scenario-based foresight, scenarios from different perspectives generate open-minded conversations in which advisers can see that

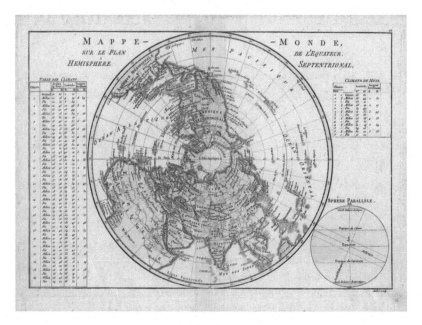

Fig. 3.1 World map projection with the North Pole in the centre, Rigobert Bonne, 1780

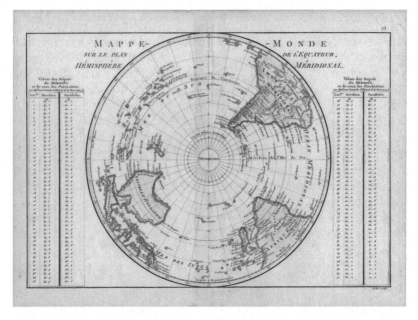

Fig. 3.2 World map projection with the South Pole in the centre, Rigobert Bonne, 1780

they need to reconsider some of their assumptions, which makes a policy problem clearer.

3.4   STEEPED: A SCHEMA FOR EXPLORING THE FUTURE FROM 360 DEGREES

A scientific foresight investigation begins with the technical horizon scan (Sect. 3.1.1), which explains the complexities of the policy issue on the basis of the latest evidence, and considers possible solutions, if the issue is a problem, or possible applications, if it is a techno-scientific development. If the latter, advisers then envision the development's possible societal impacts in explorative scenarios. These are the bases of foresight conversations with stakeholders and various experts. Advisers lead foresight conversations so that conversants look at the development from different angles.

Different institutions use different but similar schemes to do this, such as STEEP, STEEPLE and PEST, all of which are comparable with a SWOT[2] analysis. A SWOT analysis, which is perhaps the most common technique for analysing the possible impacts of a new development, evaluates it on the basis of its strengths, weaknesses and the opportunities and threats it presents to identify the factors that are favourable and unfavourable to reaching one's goal. Since 2015, we at the European Parliament have used the STEEPED scheme (Van Woensel and Vrščaj 2015), which I developed for the foresight investigation of scientific and technological issues (Fig. 3.3).

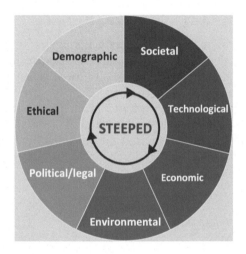

Fig. 3.3   The STEEPED scheme

It organizes an analysis along seven dimensions:

- Societal;
- Technological;
- Economic;
- Environmental;
- Political/Legal;

[2] Strengths, Weaknesses, Opportunities and Threats.

- Ethical;
- Demographic.

STEEPED helps scientific advisers to zoom out from the details of techno-scientific developments and their related policy questions and study them holistically, ensuring that we investigate their impacts in all of the areas of concern arranged under the scheme's seven dimensions. Areas investigated under different dimensions may overlap, but that is not a problem; STEEPED's aim is to prevent advisers from overlooking relevant impacts, not to organize areas into mutually exclusive categories.

3.4.1   *The Societal Perspective*

The societal dimension covers a development's impacts on lifestyles and cultural and social values. A society's cultural values are expressed in its religions, customs, traditions and rituals. Its social values provide general guidelines for members' social conduct. Their lifestyles depend on their preferences; social status, e.g., work and income; health status and abilities (talents and skills) and disabilities (limits and challenges).

So, I suggest that advisers consult the following non-exhaustive list of parameters under the 'S' of STEEPED:

- Religion;
- Ethnicity;
- Employment situation;
- Financial means;
- Health;
- Disabilities and abilities.

3.4.2   *The Technological Perspective*

The technological dimension includes the directions in which a development is evolving and its applications are diversifying, for instance, a new application's added value and the extent to which a new technology provides a new solution to a problem rather than a mere improvement on an older technology. When a technology has been developed to solve a well-defined problem, we investigate how well it works. We consider whether it has applications over and above its intended purpose. We consider its accessibility, i.e., whether and how easily individuals, institutes and companies can use it without needing new skills and training or expensive infrastructure. We consider its potential for abuse, which includes whether it can be used only for its intended purpose or has a dual use. Lastly, we consider its unmet challenges, including the need for more research, technological development and innovation (RTDI).

So, the 'T' of STEEPED covers:

- Purpose;
- Accessibility;
- Efficacy;
- Added value;
- Dual use;
- Challenges and RTDI.

3.4.3   *The Economic Perspective*

A technology's economic dimension includes its consequences for jobs, economic value, production, distribution and consumption.

A new technology can impact the labour market by creating or eliminating jobs. It can create economic value, for example, by generating revenue, increasing productivity or raising the well-being of workers. We also consider if it can be marketed immediately or if it needs new infrastructures or human resources. We also look into issues of equality. Do all of a country's or jurisdiction's individuals have equal rights and opportunities to obtain and use the technology? Does its cost relative to what purchasers are able to pay make it widely affordable?

Therefore, I suggest that under the first 'E' advisers consider:

- Job creation and loss;
- Economic value and commercialisation;
- Infrastructure and resource needs;
- Equality of access;
- Affordability.

3.4.4   The Environmental Perspective

A technology's environmental dimension includes the availability of the natural resources it requires, its interactions with natural habitats and its impacts on our biophysical environment, that is, the planet.

So, we look into a technology's impacts on air and water pollution, flora and fauna and human health. We investigate its resource efficiency, including its independence from scarce natural resources, use of renewable materials and energy and water efficiency. We consider its components' recyclability and the energy that recycling requires. Finally, we study how safe it is, which includes how safe its manufacturing process and its products and by-products are for workers and how safe it is for its users and the environment.

Therefore, I suggest looking into the following under the second 'E':

- Environmental impact;
- Natural resource use;
- Water and energy efficiency;
- Recyclability;
- Production safety;
- Product safety.

3.4.5   The Political and Legal Perspectives

A technology's political and legal dimension includes the changes in government policy, regulations and laws pertaining to, for example, employment, taxes and the environment, that it requires. It also includes market structures. For instance, does it require a specific coordination of markets (such as the European Digital Single Market for the coordination of the digital economy). We investigate systems of legal liability, for instance, for decision-making algorithms. We investigate its contribution to democracy. We consider how it impacts individuals' legal rights and civil liberties, for instance, whether certain public services are available only to citizens with access to the Internet. Lastly, I itemise geopolitical aspects as a political perspective, although these could be matched under other categories as well. Geopolitics focuses on the combination of political, geographic and economic aspects relating to a technology.

Therefore, I suggest that the 'P' include:

- Laws and regulations;
- Market structures;
- Liability;
- Democratic aspects;
- Individual rights;
- Geopolitical aspects.

3.4.6   The Ethical Perspective

A technology's ethical dimension covers its impact on a society's moral values. One of the most crucial is respect for persons, and it is essential that advisers investigate how the technology affects a society's respect for human dignity, for instance, whether it is acceptable for a democratic society to install cameras equipped with emotion recognition technology in public areas. Also important is how it affects peoples' respect for the natural environment. We investigate its impact on the autonomy of individuals, including those with disabilities. For example, will people be able to maintain their individuality if there is social pressure to use the technology. We consider whether it will be available to everybody fairly and independently of other technologies. Its potential benefits should outweigh its potential harms.

Therefore, I suggest that the third 'E' include:

- Respect for persons;
- Respect for the environment;
- Individual autonomy;
- Fair availability;
- Ratio of benefit to harm.

3.4.7   The Demographic Perspective

The demographic dimension of a technology involves its impacts on a society's social groups defined in terms of age, gender, household composition, education, occupation and geographical place of residence. The demographic dimension is distinct from the societal dimension in that the former covers statistical factors while the latter pertains to social and cultural values (Fig. 3.4).

Therefore, under the 'D' I suggest that advisers consider:

- Age;
- Gender;
- Household composition;
- Education level;
- Occupation;
- Geographical residence.

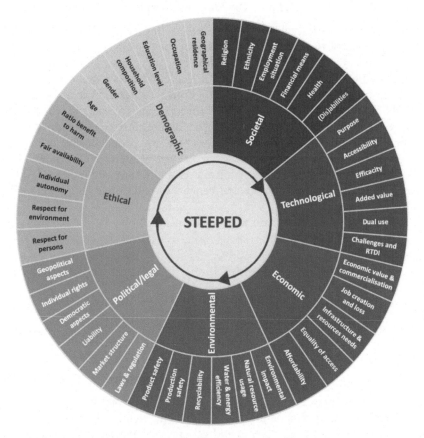

Fig. 3.4   The STEEPED scheme with all of its areas

STEEPED can be employed in several phases of the advisory project (Chapter 5). Advisers can use it in reframing policy-makers' request for advice and in assessing the evidence in the technical analysis. But its core use is in the foresight process to ensure that one investigates possible social and cross-policy (Chapter 4) impacts from the widest variety of perspectives. Had it been available at the time, the use of STEEPED probably would have prevented adoption of the biofuel policy. (See Chapter 4 for how cross-policy impact assessment can prevent such policy mistakes.)

3.5   FORESIGHT CONVERSATIONS

A foresight intervention consists in facilitated brainstorming sessions, which I call "foresight conversations", with multiple stakeholders and interdisciplinary experts. In a foresight conversation, stakeholders articulate the benefits and risks that they believe the technology under investigation will present to them. In her *Strategic Foresight Primer* (Wilkinson 2017), Angela Wilkinson describes the difference between a foresight conversation and a technical analysis of scientific evidence. In the latter, experts try to reach a consensus on what is correct and what is inaccurate in a synthesis of the evidence. In the former, advisers and experts actively listen to stakeholders in order to understand their concerns about the technology; so, there is no need for consensus on its consequences. In fact, consensus is usually not possible because stakeholders have their individual views and prejudices about the technology.

Foresight conversations should follow three basic rules:

1. They consider the technology from multiple perspectives;
2. They are interdisciplinary;
3. They include a variety of stakeholders.

I explain the benefits of (2) and (3) in the next section.

3.6   INTERDISCIPLINARY CONVERSATIONS WITH MULTIPLE STAKEHOLDERS

Interdisciplinary group thinking generates the variety of perspectives that an effective foresight investigation needs, and it enriches their elaboration, both of which sharpen advisers' thinking about policy options.

3.6.1   Interactive Thinking

According to Hugo Mercier and Dan Sperber (Mercier and Sperber 2011), individuals thinking on their own, without the benefit of input from others, can assess only their own opinions. They are both judge and jury or, rather, judge and prosecutor, which is not optimal in pursuing the truth. In *The Enigma of Reason* (Mercier and Sperber 2017), they look at 'interactionist' and 'intellectualist' reasoning. Interactionist reasoning involves looking for arguments for one's beliefs that convince others to accept them. In intellectualist reasoning, one assesses the soundness of arguments for one's beliefs with an open mind. We usually think that valid arguments establish the rationality of their conclusions and, thus, enhance an individual's decision-making, but Mercier and Sperber cite evidence that shows that people working in a group tend to reason much better than they do on their own. According to their explanation, this is because in a group we reason interactionistically. Interactionist thinking can polarize the group when its members pursue justifications for different beliefs, but it enhances the group's performance when they share the goal of justifying a particular belief, even if they have different ideas about how to justify it, because they work together to find arguments that convince outsiders.

3.6.2   Interdisciplinary Thinking About Evidence

In the *Oxford Handbook of Interdisciplinarity* (Frodeman et al. 2017), Robert Frodeman describes unidisciplinary scientific research on a problem as conducted by researchers from the same discipline working independently. He describes three types of 'cross-disciplinary integration': (1) multidisciplinarity, in which researchers from different disciplines work on the problem sequentially; (2) interdisciplinarity, in which researchers from different disciplines work independently, integrating their perspectives, concepts and methods to some degree while remaining anchored in their disciplines, and (3) transdisciplinarity, in which researchers integrate their diverse disciplines and extend the integration to find new approaches to the problem. In *The Virtual Weapon* (Kello 2017), Lucas Kello classifies cyber-theoretic research similarly: (1) unidisciplinarity, which can hinder the investigation; (2) multidisciplinarity, which recognizes the need for diverse points of view but does not integrate them, and (3) interdisciplinarity (or "transdisciplinarity" [Choi and Pak 2008]), which strives for shared insights while respecting the integrity of different disciplines. In the interdisciplinary research that Kello describes, computer scientists, political scientists, legal scholars, anthropologists and others worked together, and their awareness of each other's conceptions led them to new insights.

In *The Politics of Scientific Advice: Institutional Design for Quality Assurance* (Lentsch and Weingart 2011), Justus Lentsch and Peter Weingart recommend that advisers employ experts from multiple disciplines to assess scientific evidence. But I believe that such multidisciplinarity is inadequate for scientific policy advising and recommend interdisciplinarity instead, i.e., that researchers from different disciplines integrate the concepts and methods of their disciplines and employ the synthesis in their systems analysis of the policy issues they investigate to discover new approaches to it. A good scientific advisory study might involve natural scientists, technicians and engineers, social scientists, a philosopher and a lawyer. A psychologist is also useful for analysing clients' needs at the start, facilitating discussion in the foresight phase and steering the communication phase so that policy-makers consider the advice attentively.

3.6.3   Multiple Stakeholders

Stakeholders are those who are affected by the technology or scientific development being investigated and will be affected by or can affect the eventual policies for them. So, their views on the matter are relevant to advisers' envisioning the development's possible societal impacts and must be included. Foresight interventions are designed to do that. This is the approach of Responsible Research and Innovation (RRI) (Schomberg 2007; Stilgoe et al. 2013), which Goodin and Dryzek (2006) describe as working with 'mini-publics'.

3.6.4   Interdisciplinary, Multi-Stakeholder Group Thinking

I believe that the most effective way for advisers to conduct foresight investigations is in interdisciplinary brainstorming groups that include representatives of societal stakeholders. This method incorporates Mercier and Sperber's interactionist reasoning in an interdisciplinary conversation in which multiple stakeholders participate. For advisers to understand the views of society adequately, it is important that the team of investigators is a mix of genders, ages and scientific disciplines and that the stakeholders' representatives selected for the foresight study are a mix of the former two.

3.6.5   *Stakeholder Analysis*

A stakeholder analysis identifies who is affected by the issue under investigation and who will be affected by and who can affect the policy decision and then selects individuals representing these stakeholders to express their opinions and emotions about the development and policy options for it in the foresight conversation. There are many ways to categorise stakeholders, and the method that advisers employ in the stakeholder analysis is a determinant of the quality of the foresight study. In 'Biofuel Production: Stakeholders' Identification' (2014), Fawzy and Componation describe a method for classifying stakeholders in biofuel policy in terms of a list of typologies, which resulted in 36 types of stakeholders. So, stakeholder analysis can be complicated and time consuming.

But simpler methods are adequate for conducting a foresight study. The simplest stakeholder analysis applies the STEEPED scheme. Consider our advisory work at the European Parliament on the policy issue of precision agriculture. Our stakeholder analysis identified the relevant societal groups on the basis of the six main components of our project: (1) developing an overview of agricultural production in the EU, (2) developing an overview of business models of farming in Europe, (3) identifying the trends in precision agriculture in the EU, (4) analysing the economics and regulation of digitalisation in precision agriculture, (5) analysing the environmental impact of precision agriculture and (6) identifying the skills that workers in precision agriculture need. We applied STEEPED to these, and the resulting stakeholders were academics, farmers' associations, environmental NGOs, the agricultural machinery industry and regulators.

3.7   THE ROLE OF BACKCASTING IN THE FORESIGHT STUDY

In order to apply its results, a foresight intervention must include a backcasting or roadmap for arriving at a certain possible future starting from the current situation. Backcasting is the phase of the advising process where the *corpus* of applicable legislative texts and related documents (see Fig. 1.2), the last input from the science-policy ecosystem, enters. Scientific advisers can target possible futures extracted from the scenarios they developed in the foresight conversations. These can be desirable futures that the backcastings show policy-makers how to reach or undesirable futures they show them how to avoid. Policy-makers decide policy on the basis of the back-castings in conjunction with the technical report on the current state of affairs and the conclusions of the foresight study.

In sequential backcasting, the current situation is compared with a possible future in order to construct one or more paths to it. The analysis can reveal a number of phases, each consisting in a series of steps taken over the course of 10–20 years, depending on the current technology and legislation. Possible futures for, say, 2035 are:

- Cultured meat is the norm;
- Self-driving vehicles are everywhere;
- Drones provide all kinds of services, from delivering goods to inspecting skyscrapers;
- Available drinking water is reduced by 50%;
- All sources of electricity are renewable and sustainable.

I will use the first two to illustrate the backcasting process.

3.7.1 Illustration: Backcasting to Cultured Meat

Backcasting to an envisioned future scenario should anticipate necessary changes in the law, and according to Jens Van Steerteghem (Van Woensel and Van Steerteghem 2019) cultured meat will have to comply with the European Food Safety Authority's (EFSA) regulations for novel foods. And there will have to be labelling regulations. Making cultured meat the norm by 2035 may require greater investment in research and development and measures to move livestock farmers to other kinds of climate- and environment-friendly agricultural production that contribute to global food resilience. In addition, since food is an emotional subject, meeting the goal may require ways to convince consumers to buy cultured meat.

3.7.2 Illustration: Backcasting to Self-Driving Cars

Some believe that self-driving cars will provide continually well-regulated traffic with significantly fewer casualties. Others do not trust the algorithms or the engineering that will be used or think that the cars will be liable to being hacked. A backcasting identifies steps that can be taken to ensure the adequacy of their software, engineering and cyber-security.

The resolution of the European Parliament (Civil Law Rules on Robotics 2017) on civil law for robotics (Sect. 3.8) already covers these issues. In the resolution, the Members of the European Parliament (MEPs) asked the European Commission to propose rules for the development of robotics and artificial intelligence (including self-driving cars) that would allow full exploitation of their economic potential and guarantee a standard level of safety and security. They noted that several countries plan to enact regulatory standards for robots and argued that the EU should take the lead in setting the standards so that it will not have to follow those set by non-member countries. After comparing the current regulations on robotics with the regulatory needs in a future with self-driving cars, the MEPs stressed the urgent need to draft legislation that will clarify liability issues. They also called for a mandatory insurance scheme and a supplementary fund to ensure that victims of accidents involving driverless cars are fully compensated. They asked the European Commission to consider eventually creating a specific legal status for robots that will establish who is liable for the damage they cause. And they urged the European Commission to monitor how the rapid development of robots affects the labour market by creating, displacing and eliminating jobs.

The MEPs stressed that the growing use of robotics raises ethical issues, for example, about privacy and safety. They proposed a voluntary ethical code of conduct for robotics researchers and designers to ensure that they work in accord with ethical standards and that robot design and use respect human dignity.

Finally, MEPs asked the Commission to consider creating a European agency for robotics and artificial intelligence to provide public authorities technical, ethical and regulatory expertise. This would ensure that policymakers in the wide area of robotics and artificial intelligence would always have access to the most up-to-date scientific advice.

3.8   THE FORESIGHT PROCESS IN PRACTICE

> Foresight is the assembling of collective intelligence for anticipating future events.

There is no single way to conduct a foresight study. In the European Parliament's scientific advising service (STOA), we have incorporated foresight since January 2015 and adjusted our practice in accord with our experiences. Although variations are possible, scientific foresight will usually include the following six phases:

1. **Report on the current state of affairs**
   One should always start with the current scientific evidence about the techno-scientific issue being investigated. This can be in the form of a technology assessment study or an in-depth report by a European agency or international organisation. This phase is entirely evidence-based and, ideally, the evidence has been peer-reviewed. The experts who prepare the report should represent a range of disciplines.

2. **Stakeholder analysis**
   To compose the stakeholder group, one can conduct a stakeholder analysis on the basis of the project's main lines of research or apply the STEEPED schema. In my experience, a good stakeholder analysis results in the selection of stakeholders with different educational backgrounds, thereby fulfilling the interdisciplinarity criterion.

3. **Envisioning possible future impacts**
   One way to explore possible future societal impacts is in a group composed of the experts who prepared the report on the current state of affairs and stakeholders' representatives. This group of 10–20 participants has three tasks:

   (1) challenge the assumptions of the experts who compiled the background report;
   (2) envision the technology's possible impacts during a facilitated foresight conversation;
   (3) investigate the opportunities and concerns of possible futures.

   These can be accomplished in one or two meetings, depending on the issue's complexity and the study's time frame.

4. **Future scenarios**
   On the basis of the possible future impacts identified in the previous phase, one imagines future scenarios and explores their opportunities and challenges in depth.

5. **Policy alternatives**
   One can derive policy alternatives from the previous four steps. Ideally, the options are varied and include the most desirable and undesirable scenarios. Advisers know from the foresight phase's brainstorming sessions which scenarios stakeholders find desirable and undesirable.
6. **Backcasting**
   The last phase is backcasting, in which one outlines roadmaps for
   reaching a desirable future and avoiding an undesirable one. This
   phase involves institutional memory, i.e., current legislation, and suggestions for new legislation that may be needed.

3.9   THE CASE OF ROBOTICS

Box 3.1 outlines the foresight study from our pilot robotics project, whose
results were extensively used by several of the European Parliament's committees and contributed to the Parliament's resolution calling on the European Commission to propose rules for robotics and artificial intelligence
(EP 2017).

Box 3.1 Steps and timeline of a STOA scientific foresight study
STOA's foresight study, 'The Ethics of Cyber-Physical Systems'

- Requested by the Committee on Legal Affairs (JURI)
- Starting point—state of the art: autumn 2015
- Envisioning impacts: January 2016
- Scenario writing: February 2016
- Exploring scenarios' challenges and opportunities: February 2016
- Backcasting, legal and ethical reflections and anticipating future chal-
  lenges and opportunities: March–June 2016
- Regular study updates to the JURI Working Group on Robotics and
  Artificial Intelligence: 2015–2016
- Publication: June 2016 (Van Woensel et al. 2017)
- Animated infographic: February 2017 (STOA 2017)

Towards the European Parliament's resolution on civil law for robotics

- Draft report (rapporteur: Mady Delvaux, S&D, LU): 31 May 2016
  (Delvaux 2016)

- Opinions of the Committees on Transport and Tourism (TRAN); Civil Liberties, Justice and Home Affairs (LIBE); Employment and Social Affairs (EMPL); Environment, Public Health and Food Safety (ENVI); Industry, Research and Energy (ITRE) and Internal Market and Consumer Protection (IMCO): between 12 October and 23 November 2016 (Boni 2016; Buşoi 2016; Charanzová 2016; Kallas 2016; Kósa 2016; Mayer 2016)
- Vote in Committee on Legal Affairs (JURI): 12 January 2017
- Committee report tabled for plenary session: 27 January 2017 (Delvaux 2017)
- Debate in EP plenary session: 15 February 2017
- Text adopted by EP (T8-0051/2017): 16 February 2017 (EP 2017)

3.10   Chapter Summary and Conclusions

Scientific foresight extends traditional technology assessment by focusing on the possible long-term societal impacts of emerging technologies, imagining explorative scenarios that take those envisaged impacts into account, exploring the challenges and opportunities in those future scenarios and, finally, backcasting these challenges and opportunities to current policy.

Scientific foresight is a way to understand the impacts that techno-scientific developments and trends will have on society and to advise policy-makers on how to anticipate them. Foresight-based policy advice assists policy-makers in making strategic decisions by describing and backcasting possible futures so that they can take steps toward some and away from others. It can also raise awareness about unavoidable futures.

Scientific advisers formulate impartial advice and communicate it impartially, for it is not their job to judge which futures are desirable and which ones are undesirable. That is what policy-makers do.

References

Banta, David. 2009. "What Is Technology Assessment?" *International Journal of Technology Assessment in Health Care* 25 (Suppl. 1): 7–9. https://doi.org/10.1017/s0266462309090333.

Boni, Michal. 2016. Opinion of the Committee on Civil Liberties, Justice and Home Affairs for the Committee on Legal Affairs with Recommendations to the Commission on Civil Law Rules on Robotics (2015/2103(INL)). Brussels: European Parliament.

Boucher, Philip. 2017. *How Blockchain Technology Could Change Our Lives: European Parliament*. Brussels: STOA, European Parliamentary Research Service.

Buşoi, Cristian-Silviu. 2016. Opinion of the Committee on the Environment, Public Health and Food Safety for the Committee on Legal Affairs with Recommendations to the Commission on Civil Law Rules on Robotics (2015/2103(INL)). Brussels: European Parliament.

Centre for Strategic Futures. 2017. *Foresight: A Glossary Singapore*. Singapore: Centre for Strategic Futures.

Charanzová, Dita. 2016. Opinion of the Committee on the Internal Market and Consumer Protection for the Committee on Legal Affairs Civil Law Rules on Robotics (2015/2103(INL)). Brussels: European Parliament.

Choi, Bernard C. K., and Anita W. P. Pak. 2008. "Multidisciplinarity, Interdisciplinarity, and Transdisciplinarity in Health Research, Services, Education and Policy: 3. Discipline, Inter-discipline Distance, and Selection of Discipline." *Clinical and Investigative Medicine* 31 (1). https://doi.org/10.25011/cim.v31i1.3140.

Civil Law Rules on Robotics P8_TA(2017)0051 C.F.R. 2017. http://www.europarl.europa.eu/doceo/document/TA-8-2017-0051_EN.pdf.

Conway, Maree, and Chris Stewart. 2005. *Creating and Sustaining Social Foresight in Australia: A Review of Government Foresight*. Melbourne: Swinburne Press.

Decker, Michael, and Miltos Ladikas, eds. 2004. *Bridges Between Science, Society and Policy: Technology Assessment—Methods and Impacts*. New York: Springer.

Delvaux, Mady. 2016. Draft Report with Recommendations to the Commission on Civil Law Rules on Robotics (2015/2103(INL)). Brussels: European Parliament. http://www.europarl.europa.eu/sides/getDoc.do?pubRef=-//EP//NONSGML%2BCOMPARL%2BPE-582.443%2B01%2BDOC%2BPDF%2BV0//EN.

Delvaux, Mady. 2017. Report with Recommendations to the Commission on Civil Law Rules on Robotics (2015/2103(INL)). Brussels: European Parliament. http://www.europarl.europa.eu/doceo/document/A-8-2017-0005_EN.pdf?redirect.

EP. 2017. European Parliament Resolution of 16 February 2017 with Recommendations to the Commission on Civil Law Rules on Robotics (2015/2103(INL)). Civil Law Rules on Robotics (P8_TA(2017)0051). http://www.europarl.europa.eu/sides/getDoc.do?pubRef=-//EP//NONSGML+TA+P8-TA-2017-0051+0+DOC+PDF+V0//EN.

Fawzy, Mostafa, and Paul Componation. 2014. "Biofuel Production: Stakeholders' Identification." *Journal of Management & Engineering Integration* 7 (1): 15–22.

Frodeman, Robert, Julie Thompson Klein, and Roberto C. S. Pacheco, eds. 2017. *The Oxford Handbook of Interdisciplinarity.* 2nd ed. Oxford: Oxford University Press.

Georghiou, Luke, Jennifer Cassingena Harper, Michael Keenan, Ian Miles, and Rafael Popper, eds. 2009. *The Handbook of Technology Foresight.* Cheltenham, UK: Edward Elgar.

Goodin, Robert, and John Dryzek. 2006. "Deliberative Impacts: The Macro-Political Uptake of Mini-Publics." *Politics & Society* 34 (2): 219–244. https://doi.org/10.1177/0032329206288152.

Government Office for Science (UK). 2017. *The Futures Toolkit: Tools for Futures Thinking and Foresight Across the UK Government.* London: Government Office for Science.

Kahane, Adam. 2012. *Transformative Scenario Planning: Working Together to Change the Future.* San Francisco: Berrett-Koehler Publishers.

Kallas, Kaja. 2016. Opinion of the Committee on Industry, Research and Energy for the Committee on Legal Affairs with Recommendations to the Commission on Civil Law Rules on Robotics (2015/2103(INL)). European Parliament.

Kello, Lucas. 2017. *The Virtual Weapon and International Order.* New Haven: Yale University Press.

Kósa, Ádam. 2016. Opinion of the Committee on Employment and Social Affairs for the Committee on Legal Affairs with Recommendations to the Commission on Civil Law Rules on Robotics (2015/2103(INL)). European Parliament.

Lentsch, Justus, and Peter Weingart. 2011. *The Politics of Scientific Advice: Institutional Design for Quality Assurance.* Cambridge: Cambridge University Press.

Mayer, Georg. 2016. Opinion of the Committee on Transport and Tourism for the Committee on Legal Affairs with Recommendations to the Commission on Civil Law Rules on Robotic (2015/2103(INL)). European Parliament.

Mercier, Hugo, and Dan Sperber. 2011. "Why Do Humans Reason? Arguments for an Argumentative Theory." *Behavioral and Brain Sciences* 34 (2): 57–74. https://doi.org/10.1017/s0140525x10000968.

Mercier, Hugo, and Dan Sperber. 2017. *The Enigma of Reason: A New Theory of Human Understanding.* London: Allen Lane.

Schomberg, René Von. 2007. *From the Ethics of Technology Towards an Ethics of Knowledge Policy & Knowledge Assessment.* Luxembourg: EU Publications.

Schroeder, Karl. 2011. www.kschroeder.com/weblog/after-prediction, consulted 1 January 2019.

Schwartz, Peter. 1998. *The Art of the Long View: Planning for the Future in an Uncertain World.* New York: Wiley.

Shell International Ltd. 2008. *Scenarios: An Explorer's Guide.* Retrieved from https://www.shell.com/.

Stilgoe, J., R. Owen, and P. Macnaghten. 2013. "Developing a Framework for Responsible Innovation." *Research Policy* 42 (9): 1568–1580. https://doi.org/10.1016/j.respol.2013.05.008.

STOA. 2016. *Ethical Aspects of Cyber-Physical Systems: A Scientific Foresight Study.* Edited by Lieve Van Woensel, Christian Kurrer, and Mihalis Kritikos. Brussels: STOA, European Parliamentary Research Service.

STOA. 2017. *The Ethics of Cyber-Physical Systems (CPS): Animated Infographics.* Retrieved from http://www.europarl.europa.eu/thinktank/infographics/robotics/public/index.html.

Swierstra, Tsjalling. 2015. "Identifying the Normative Challenges Posed by Technology's 'Soft' Impacts." *Etikk i Praksis: Nordic Journal of Applied Ethics* 9 (1): 5–20. https://doi.org/10.5324/eip.v9i1.1838.

Swierstra, Tsjalling, and Hedwig Frederica te Molder. 2012. "Risk and Soft Impacts." In *Handbook of Risk Theory: Epistemology, Decision Theory, Ethics, and Social Implications of Risk*, edited by Sabine Roeser, Rafeala Hillerbrand, Martin Peterson, and Per Sandin, 1050–1066. Dordrecht: Springer.

Taleb, Nassim Nicholas. 2010. *The Black Swan: The Impact of the Highly Improbable.* 2nd ed. New York: Random House Trade Paperbacks.

van Asselt, Marjolein, Susan van 't Klooster, Phillip van Notten, and Livia Smits. 2010. *Foresight in Action: Developing Policy-Oriented Scenarios.* Washington, DC: Earthscan.

Van der Heijden, Kees. 2005. *Scenarios: The Art of Strategic Conversation.* 2nd ed. Chichester: Wiley.

Van Woensel, Lieve, and Jens Van Steerteghem. 2019. *What if We Didn't Need Cows for Our Beef?* Brussels: European Parliament Research Service.

Van Woensel, Lieve, and Darja Vrščaj. 2015. *Towards Scientific Foresight in the European Parliament: In-Depth Analysis.* Brussels: European Parliamentary Research Service.

Wilkinson, Angela. 2017. *Strategic Foresight Primer.* Luxembourg: European Political Strategy Centre.

Wilkinson, Angela, and Roland Kupers. 2014. *The Essence of Scenarios: Learning from the Shell Experience.* Amsterdam: Amsterdam University Press.

CHAPTER 4

Systems Thinking and Assessing Cross-Policy Impacts

Abstract This chapter offers scientific advisers practical ways to avoid overlooking unintended effects of the policy options they formulate on the society as well as on other policies. It describes ways for advisers to conduct cross-policy analyses in order to avoid conflicting policy actions that will be regretted later, and it offers a tool for conducting these analyses, namely, the doughnut scheme.

Keywords Systems analysis · Policy assessment · Doughnut scheme · Cross-Policy assessment

This chapter gives practical guidelines for the use of systems analysis in strategically designing a scientific advisory project and assessing its outcomes. I describe the practical uses of two types of systems thinking: outward and inward. Outward systems thinking guides the analysis, which I described in Sect. 1.4, in which advisers zoom out from the policy-maker's original question to a full picture of the scope of the issue or problem, including its stakeholders, on the basis of which they plan the inputs to their research. The central theme of the chapter is inward systems thinking. In their inward systems analysis, advisers assess the policy options they articulate for their unintended effects on society and on other policies, both global and local. I develop a framework for advisers to identify existing policies potentially in conflict with the policy options they consider,

© The Author(s) 2020
L. Van Woensel, *A Bias Radar for Responsible Policy-Making*,
St Antony's Series, https://doi.org/10.1007/978-3-030-32126-0_4

which ensures that they do not overlook any, and conduct cross-policy analyses on the two to avoid policy decisions that will be regretted later. It was the biofuel policy's unanticipated effects on land use that stimulated me to develop this framework. I illustrate inward systems analysis with an imaginary example of a policy for increasing the use of electric cars. I also consider various ways to formulate policy options for reaching a desired future and avoiding undesirable ones. My framework for inward systems analysis was inspired by Kate Raworth's Doughnut (2017); it is a doughnut scheme for identifying and assessing possible cross-policy impacts.

4.1   SYSTEMS ANALYSIS AND SCIENTIFIC ADVICE

Two good books on practical systems thinking are Peter Senge's *The Fifth Discipline: The Art and Practice of the Learning Organization* (Senge 2006) and Donella Meadows's *Thinking in Systems: A Primer* (Meadows and Wright 2008). Meadows was one of the authors of the first well-known scenario-based foresight study, *The Limits to Growth: A Report for the Club of Rome's Project on the Predicament of Mankind* (Robinson et al. 1973), and of *Limits to Growth: The 30-Year Update* (Meadows et al. 2005). She describes a system as an interconnected set of elements coherently organised to achieve some end. In our case, the end is the policy options that advisers recommend to decision-makers. Senge characterizes systems thinking as a way to understand the forces acting on a system and the interrelationships among its component that together determine the system's behaviour. For example, among the forces affecting the behaviour of the science-policy ecosystem are those exerted by the uncontrolled input, such as cognitive biases, interest groups and actors' personal environments.

In *Making Better Decisions Using Systems Thinking* (Schaveling and Bryan 2018), Jaap Schaveling and Bill Bryan specify three variables that frame one's choices in management and daily life, namely, time (short term versus long term), scope (limited scope versus encompassing scope) and awareness (reality versus imagination). All three, at their right-hand values, frame an advisory project, as foresight systems thinking zooms out to consider the widest scope of long-term consequences of imagined possibilities. Therefore, I call this "outward systems thinking". Once advisers have been assigned an issue or problem, an outward systems analysis, zooming out to see the science-policy ecosystem as widely as necessary to ensure that it includes all of the stakeholders affecting or affected by the issue, ensures the highest-quality design of their advisory project.

STEEPED guides advisers' outward systems thinking to include:

- The possible sources of input for an investigation of the issue from all possible perspectives; the chosen source determines the sorts of scientific evidence that will be collected;
- The societal groups that are affected by the issue and will be affected by, or can affect, the eventual policy, all of which should be involved in the collection of societal evidence in the foresight investigation;
- The relevant interest groups;
- The relevant institutional memory, i.e., legislative texts, to see where policy options can incorporate existing law.

Thus, the outward systems analysis locates the issue in the whole science-policy ecosystem.

4.2   Inward Systems Thinking: Cross-Policy Impact Assessment

As Schaveling and Bryan argue in *Making Better Decisions Using Systems Thinking*, systems thinking can anticipate and avoid unintended side-effects of policy decisions. In their inward systems analysis, advisers zoom in on each of the policy options they formulate to ensure that they have not overlooked any of its unintended impacts on society and other policies. So, I now suppose that we conducted an outward systems analysis to design the project and have developed a set of policy options on the basis of its results. To ensure that the options are of the highest quality, we must conduct an inward systems analysis to assess the impacts on society and on other policies, both global and local.

Let me again use biodiesel promotion as an example of a policy option. Since diesel emits less CO_2 than gasoline, this option may seem effective for tackling climate change (a global issue). So, it may have the societal impact of signalling, incorrectly, that the use of diesel is preferable. However, applying STEEPED reveals the health consequences of the particulate matter in diesel exhaust (a local issue). It also reveals the unintended consequence of changing land use, which would jeopardise food security

Fig. 4.1   The Sustainable Development Goals set by the United Nations

(a global issue with particular implications for developing countries and people living in poverty). Both consequences contradict the intended effects of other policies.

4.2.1   *Exploration of Possible Global-Policy Conflicts with the UN's SDGs*

I recommend that advisers use the 17 Sustainable Development Goals (SDGs) of the United Nations' '2030 Agenda for Sustainable Development' (UN 2015) as a checklist to identify possibly affected policies.[1] In August 2015, 193 countries agreed to the SDGs, which are listed in Box 4.1 and illustrated in the well-known Fig. 4.1.

---

[1] https://sustainabledevelopment.un.org/sdgs.

Box 4.1 The 17 Sustainable Development Goals adopted by the United Nations in 2015

1. End poverty in all its forms everywhere.
2. End hunger, achieve food security and improved nutrition and promote sustainable agriculture.
3. Ensure healthy lives and promote well-being for all at all ages.
4. Ensure inclusive and equitable quality education and promote lifelong learning opportunities for all.
5. Achieve gender equality and empower all women and girls.
6. Ensure availability and sustainable management of water and sanitation for all.
7. Ensure access to affordable, reliable, sustainable and modern energy for all.
8. Promote sustained, inclusive and sustainable economic growth, full and productive employment and decent work for all.
9. Build resilient infrastructure, promote inclusive and sustainable industrialization and foster innovation.
10. Reduce inequality within and among countries.
11. Make cities and human settlements inclusive, safe, resilient and sustainable.
12. Ensure sustainable consumption and production patterns.
13. Take urgent action to combat climate change and its impacts by regulating emissions and promoting developments in renewable energy.
14. Conserve and sustainably use the oceans, seas and marine resources for sustainable development.
15. Protect, restore and promote sustainable use of terrestrial ecosystems, sustainably manage forests, combat desertification, and halt and reverse land degradation and halt biodiversity loss.
16. Promote peaceful and inclusive societies for sustainable development, provide access to justice for all and build effective, accountable and inclusive institutions at all levels.
17. Strengthen the means of implementation and revitalize the global partnership for sustainable development.

4.2.2   Illustration: Incentivise Consumers to Purchase Electric Cars

I illustrate the process of assessing a policy option's impact on society and other policies with a hypothetical policy for increasing energy efficiency by offering financial incentives to Europeans to buy electric cars.[2]

The first phase of the scientific advising project is the technical horizon scan. A quick exploration of various sources (Waide and Brunner 2011; Cohn 2018; European Environment Agency 2016, 2018; International Energy Agency 2018, 2019; International Energy Agency and International Council on Clean Transportation 2019) reveals the following elements:

- Cars' internal combustion engines are not energy efficient. In real-life fuel-to-wheels use, gasoline vehicles use only about 20% of their fuel's energy content and diesel vehicles about 25%. The most efficient diesel engines could reach up to 40% energy efficiency at their optimal operation point. In 'Electric vehicles in Europe', the European Environment Agency estimates that electric vehicles convert around 80% of the energy they use. The usable energy is stored in the battery, i.e. not including the battery efficiency. Overall, the EEA estimates electric car efficiency at around 65% compared to 20–25% for a conventional internal combustion vehicle.
- It is estimated that replacing internal combustion cars with electric cars would reduce the total energy consumption of cars by two-thirds.
- If electric cars replace 90% of internal combustion cars by 2030, the electricity supply would have to increase by around 20–25% by then.

Now, we must identify existing policies that the option might affect if it became policy. First, we think about its effects on global policies. We quickly run through the 17 SDGs, consider any specific targets that are matters of policy and list all of the possible connections and concerns.

---

[2] N.B. The illustration is very simple and does not include the collection of full, impartial and high-quality evidence or a foresight investigation. In a real case, advisers would gather the scientific evidence from recent research conducted by reputable knowledge centres, such as the International Energy Agency and the European Environment Agency.

- SDG 7. Ensure access to affordable, reliable, sustainable and modern energy for all:
  The option would require significant efforts to increase the production of electricity and the share of renewables in its production.
- SDG 9. Build resilient infrastructure, promote inclusive and sustainable industrialization and foster innovation:
  The option would have to be combined with an increase in the infrastructure for producing renewable and other electricity and with the construction of a network of fast charging stations. It would also foster innovation in the transition to battery-free decarbonised transportation, such as hydrogen cars, and soon result in decarbonisation through the use of electric vehicles.
- SDG 10. Reduce inequality within and among countries:
  Within countries, income inequality may increase, assuming that the low-income population cannot afford electric cars and that tax payers pay for the incentives for those who can afford them. Use of electric cars also requires available space for charging their batteries. Inequality may increase between countries whose citizens can afford electric cars and countries where the minerals for their batteries are mined, which are often conflict areas in Africa.
- SDG 11. Make cities and human settlements inclusive, safe, resilient and sustainable:
  Replacing a high proportion of internal combustion cars with electric ones would drastically reduce air pollution by particulate matter and its effects on urban populations.
- SDG 12. Ensure sustainable consumption and production patterns:
  Providing citizens incentives to buy electric cars might reinforce private car ownership and thereby hamper any considerable behavioural changes that could be achieved by, for example, combining shared cars and public transportation. Furthermore, an electric vehicle is only as green as the electricity that feeds its battery. The policy option would require significant efforts to increase the production of electricity from renewable—ideally, inexhaustible—sources. Some authors claim that on average the production of an electric vehicle uses twice the energy and contributes twice as much to global warming than does the production of an internal combustion car (Eckart 2017). Whether or not this is true should be determined.

- SDG 13. Take urgent action to combat climate change and its impacts:
  Promoting the use of electric cars contributes to this goal, provided that they are charged with renewable electricity.
- SDG 15. Protect, restore and promote sustainable use of terrestrial ecosystems, sustainably manage forests, combat desertification, and halt and reverse land degradation and halt biodiversity loss:
  Promoting the use of electric cars contributes to this goal, provided that the electricity they use is ideally from renewable and inexhaustible sources.
- SDG 16. Promote peaceful and inclusive societies for sustainable development, provide access to justice for all and build effective, accountable and inclusive institutions at all levels:
  The minerals required for electric cars' batteries are rare and available in only a few areas of the world, and securing their supply does not promote peaceful and inclusive societies. Most are mined in conflict areas, such as the Katanga district of the Democratic Republic of Congo, which supplies around 60% of the world's cobalt. Research shows that cobalt mining endangers miners and the environment (Blijweert 2018). Research also shows that mining companies use child labour and the communities they employ live in deplorable environmental conditions. The producers, owners and users of electric cars may have a shared responsibility to improve living and working conditions in these areas. Research into alternative battery technologies should be accelerated as should research into other types of carbon-emission-free cars, such as hydrogen cars, for which the fuel can be produced locally from renewable and inexhaustible sources.

In this way, consideration of the SDGs reveals some of the policy option's possible intended and unintended impacts on existing global policies.

4.2.3   Identification of Possible Cross-Policy Impacts at the Level of the EU

It is on the basis of the same considerations that we begin to investigate the policy option's possible conflicts with EU policies. At this point, we must consider the full list of the European Parliament's competences (Box 4.2).

Box 4.2 List of the European Parliament's competences

Agriculture	Education	Human Rights	Research
Budgetary Control	Employment	Industry	Rural Development
Budgets	Energy	Internal Market	Security
Civil Liberties	Environment	International Trade	Social Affairs
Constitutional Affairs	Fisheries	Justice	Tourism
Consumer Protection	Food Safety	Legal Affairs	Transport
Culture	Foreign Affairs	Petitions	Women's Rights
Defence	Gender Equality	Public health	
Development	Home Affairs	Regional Development	

We proceed on this basis, guided by STEEPED. For example:

- **Consumer protection**: Will consumers be able to sell their old cars at reasonable prices? Will appropriate charging infrastructure be available? Will sufficient electricity be supplied at a reasonable price?
- **Education**: There will be a need to re-train people in the car maintenance sector.
- **Development**: It will be necessary to improve working and living conditions in countries where the minerals needed for electric car batteries are mined.
- **Employment**: We will have to investigate the possible consequences for the job market.
- **Energy**: A large number of electric cars will require a large increase in electricity production, and that will require a large increase in the infrastructure for producing and storing renewable electricity.
- **Environment**: How can sufficient renewable electricity be generated from inexhaustible sources? What about battery recyclability? What will happen with the internal combustion cars? How can the EU contribute to eco-friendly mining of the necessary minerals?

- **Industry**: A dense network of charging stations will have to be constructed. Dependency on cobalt and nickel for the production of batteries must be addressed.
- **International trade**: Most current battery producers are not based in the EU; production will be highly dependent on minerals from non-EU countries.
- **Public health**: A decrease in particulate air pollution will improve the air quality in urban areas; mining will probably worsen public health in the (non-EU) regions where the necessary minerals are located.
- **Research**: Research into powerful charging stations; alternative batteries and battery-free zero-carbon-emission vehicles, such as hydrogen cars, must all be increased.
- **Transport**: The option would be a step towards clean transportation; it would require construction of high-power charging infrastructure.

4.3   REITERATING THE PROCESS: THE DOUGHNUT SCHEME

To ensure that advisers anticipate all of our policy options' possible cross-policy impacts so that their advice to policy-makers is future-proof, I recommend that they repeat parts of the previous two analyses until they turn up no new concerns. Reiteration is included in the feedback loops of systems analysis (see Fig. 1.3). I also recommend that they now use STEEPED to look for possible impacts at the policy level at which they have been asked for advice. Once they have identified some, they can reiterate the foresight analysis with relevant stakeholders.

Next, they employ the doughnut in Fig. 4.2, which was inspired by Kate Raworth's Doughnut (Raworth 2017). I developed the scheme to avoid the cross-policy impacts that lead to regrettable policy decisions, which is how several interviewees characterized the biofuel policy. They apply the doughnut to each policy option on a white board with STEEPED in the centre and the option's potentially related policies in a circle around it. The doughnut exercise requires the participation of an expert in each associated policy.

In practice, reiteration of the exercise leads to creative policy solutions.

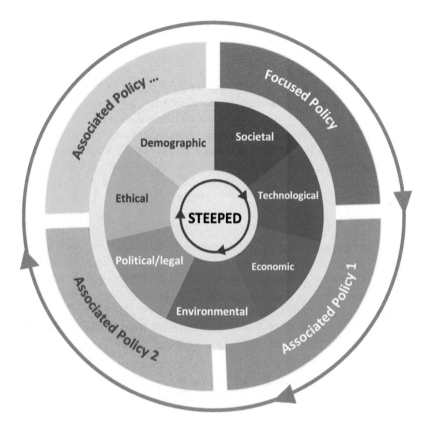

Fig. 4.2 The doughnut scheme for assessing possible cross-policy impacts

4.4   Reflections on Alternative Ways to Reach a Goal

In this final section, I describe how policy-makers can consider different kinds of instruments that lead to the same policy goal. I also give an example of how advisers can circumvent blind spots by thinking out of the box.

4.4.1   'Carrots, Sticks and Sermons'

Policy-makers can achieve a specific goal by implementing any of a number of different policy instruments. *Carrots, Sticks and Sermons: Policy Instruments and Their Evaluation* (Bemelmans-Videc et al. 1998), written by a policy-maker, a policy adviser and a public administrator, analyses three different types of policy instruments, which they call *"carrots"*, *"sticks"* and *"sermons"*, that is, economic incentives, regulations and information. Considering the three is useful in comparing alternative ways to reach a policy goal. For instance, to increase private ownership of electric cars, a carrot would be financial incentives; a stick would be a tax on diesel cars or a ban on them in certain areas and a sermon would be informing owners of diesel cars about particulate matter in their exhaust. Carrots are usually financed publicly, and, as one interviewee stated, as taxpayers, citizens are stakeholders in such a policy and might judge each option for such a policy on the basis of its consequences for their tax liability. Combining financial incentives with penalties for internal combustion cars penalizes citizens who cannot afford an electric car, prevents them from using their cars in banned areas and makes them contribute to those who can afford them. So, carrots and sticks must be carefully thought through when preparing policy options.

4.4.2   Policy Options that Stay Within the Limits Versus Those that Go Beyond Them

Consider advisers investigating the possibility of the sea level rising faster than climate scientists have estimated. They can advise taking mitigating or adaptive measures. Or they can advise drastic reform.

4.4.2.1   Strategy 1: Lessening Climate Change (Mitigation)

Mitigating policy options include any combination of measures for reducing or stabilizing the levels of heat-trapping greenhouse gases in the atmosphere and investing in Carbon Capture and Storage (CCS) technologies to reduce greenhouse-gas emissions. A STEEPED analysis will inform the advisers of the constraints, limitations and impacts of such measures, such as necessary changes in citizens' behaviour.

4.4.2.2 Strategy 2: Protecting Coastal Areas (Adaptation)

Coastal flooding caused by a rise in the sea level can impact vital facilities, such as for supplying energy, transportation and health care, but advisers can envision ways to adapt society to the increased risk, for example, coastal flood-control infrastructure. This might require gigantic investment and behavioural changes. Again, a STEEPED analysis will inform them of the constraints, limitations and impacts of those measures, and it may reveal doubts about their efficacy and timeliness.

4.4.2.3 Strategy 3: Organizing the World to Be Independent of the Sea Level (Reform)

Humans don't like change (as in option 1) or uncertainty (as in 1 and 2). Therefore, advisers could think about a world where one can do what one wants to without having to worry about catastrophic events not under one's control. For example, they can bring together a group of experts to brainstorm scenarios about new ways of living in newly designed environments, in which the problem is under control. Some people already do this, for example, Elon Musk with his plans to colonise Mars, but scenarios without concerns about rising sea levels would be more easily realized and would not require so much new technology; they would be closer to how we live now. For instance, we could construct communities that float on the oceans and include the water, food and infrastructure that we are used to (see Fig. 4.3). A STEEPED analysis of this scenario would identify its requirements and concerns, such as how floating societies could be self-supporting, how they could secure energy and drinking water, how they could organise farming and food processing and how their sovereignty would have to be rethought. Then, the backcasting becomes an action plan, a roadmap with concrete milestones.

I include this example to illustrate that one should not always focus on limitations. That is an attention bias, and it creates blind spots that hide innovative solutions to a problem. By systematically asking 'So what?' when confronted with well-documented limitations, one can sometimes think beyond them instead of staying within them. And this may stimulate creative reflection and ingenious solutions for humankind.

Fig. 4.3 A scenario of a new way of living adapted to climate change and a higher sea level, *Floating community on the ocean with floating farm and floating energy production (Artist: Peter Van Woensel)*

4.5   CHAPTER SUMMARY AND CONCLUSIONS

The assessment of possible cross-policy impacts substantially enhances the quality of policy advice.

To avoid policy actions that will be regretted later, scientific advisers should conduct a cross-policy impact assessment for each of the policy options they formulate. This involves identifying the existing policies that each policy option may affect and analysing the possible impacts.

Advisers can identify such global policies by scanning the United Nations' Sustainable Development Goals (SDGs). Next, they can consider the main competences of the policy level at which they are working (e.g., the competences of the European Parliament). Once they have identified the relevant policies, they employ STEEPED to conduct a cross-policy impact assessment for each of their policy options. Reiterating the process can substantially enhance the value of their recommendations. The doughnut scheme is a tool for avoiding undesirable side-effects of policy choices, leading advisers through STEEPED-based impact analyses of each individual policy option on the related policies identified.

Different types of policy instruments, 'carrots, sticks and sermons' (Bemelmans-Videc et al. 1998), can be used to reach a specific goal.

Advisers usually devise paths towards a desirable future or away from an undesirable future. However, some undesirable futures may be unavoidable. Therefore, they should sometimes envision policy options for undesirable but unavoidable futures.

REFERENCES

Bemelmans-Videc, Marie-Louise, Ray C. Rist, and Evert Vedung. 1998. *Carrots, Sticks & Sermons: Policy Instruments & Their Evaluation*. New Brunswick, NJ: Transaction Publishers.

Blijweert, Dirk. 2018. "Scientists Reveal the Hidden Costs of Cobalt Mining in DR Congo." *Physics.org*. https://phys.org/news/2018-09-scientists-reveal-hidden-cobalt-dr.html. Accessed July 19, 2019.

Cohn, Roger. 2018. "Europe Now Has One Million Electric Vehicles on the Road." *Yale Environment 360*. https://e360.yale.edu/digest/europe-now-has-one-million-electric-vehicles-on-the-road. Accessed February 3, 2019.

Eckart, Jonathan 2017. "Batteries Can Be Part of the Fight Against Climate Change—If We Do These Five Things." *World Economic Forum*. https://

www.weforum.org/agenda/2017/11/battery-batteries-electric-cars-carbon-sustainable-power-energy/. Accessed November 28, 2017.

European Environment Agency. 2016. *Electric Vehicles in Europe*. København, Denmark: European Environment Agency. https://www.eea.europa.eu/publications/electric-vehicles-in-europe/.

European Environment Agency. 2018. *Final Energy Consumption by Mode of Transport*. København, Denmark: European Environment Agency. https://www.eea.europa.eu/data-and-maps/indicators/transport-final-energy-consumption-by-mode/assessment-9.

International Energy Agency. 2019. *Fuel Economy in Major Car Markets: Technology and Policy Drivers 2005–2017*. https://webstore.iea.org.

International Energy Agency. 2018. *Energy Efficiency 2018—Analysis and Outlooks to 2040*. Paris. https://webstore.iea.org/market-report-series-energy-efficiency-2018.

International Energy Agency and International Council on Clean Transportation. 2019. *Fuel Economy in Major Car Markets*. Paris: International Energy Agency.

Meadows, Donella H., and Diana Wright. 2008. *Thinking in Systems: A Primer*. White River Junction, Vermont: Chelsea Green Publishing.

Meadows, Donella H., Jørgen Randers, and Dennis L. Meadows. 2005. *Limits to Growth: The 30-Year Update*. 3rd rev., expanded and updated ed. London: Earthscan.

Raworth, Kate. 2017. *Doughnut Economics: Seven Ways to Think Like a 21st Century Economist*. White River Junction, Vermont: Chelsea Green.

Robinson, Warren, Donella H. Meadows, Dennis L. Meadows, Jørgen Randers, and William W. Behrens. 1973. *The Limits to Growth: A Report for the Club of Rome's Project on the Predicament of Mankind*. New York: Universe.

Schaveling, Jaap, and Bill Bryan. 2018. *Making Better Decisions Using Systems Thinking: How to Stop Firefighting, Deal with Root Causes and Deliver Permanent Solutions*. Cham, Switzerland: Palgrave Macmillan.

Senge, Peter M. 2006. *The Fifth Discipline: The Art and Practice of the Learning Organization*. Rev. and updated ed. London: Random House Business Books.

United Nations. 2015. "Transforming Our World: The 2030 Agenda for Sustainable Development, Resolution 70/1, UN Doc. A/RES/70/1." September 25, 2015. https://www.un.org/ga/search/view_doc.asp?symbol=A/RES/70/1&Lang=E.

Waide, Paul, and Conrad U. Brunner. 2011. *Energy-Efficiency Policy Opportunities for Electric Motor-Driven Systems*. Paris: International Energy Agency.

CHAPTER 5

Towards Responsible Scientific Advice: Painting the Complete Picture

Abstract This chapter summarizes the scientific advisory process by presenting a model that combines all of the considerations and tools previously described. The model starts with a holistic approach to the scientific advisory process by zooming out through a systems analysis to get a broad picture of a policy problem within the entire science-policy ecosystem. It combines system analysis with bias checks to raise awareness of possible biases throughout the ecosystem, multi-disciplinary and multi-perspective STEEPED explorations, foresight thinking involving multiple stakeholders, cross-policy analysis and the quality control of evidence. The model aims to ensure a proper balance among the scientific evidence and the other inputs that bear on policy decisions. Lastly, the chapter includes reflections on the issue of trusting science and scientific advisers.

Keywords Responsible Scientific Advice (RSA) · Scientific advice · Policy advice · Science-policy ecosystem · Policy · Scientific foresight

In this chapter, I describe the overall scientific advisory process, summarizing those phases I have already discussed and describing those I have not yet portrayed. First, I summarize how to conduct an advisory project holistically, identifying its scope and zooming out to see how it relates to the entire science-policy ecosystem. Second, I elaborate on the sources of input:

© The Author(s) 2020   85
L. Van Woensel, *A Bias Radar for Responsible Policy-Making*,
St Antony's Series, https://doi.org/10.1007/978-3-030-32126-0_5

scientific evidence, information sources that influence public opinion and legislative texts. I also reflect on the limits of science. Third, I summarize the foresight process. Fourth, I briefly explain how these phases contribute to articulating and assessing policy options and devising backcastings to alternative futures. Fifth, I explain the communication of scientific advice, the last phase of an advisory project, and make recommendations for doing it efficiently and responsibly. In the process, I summarize what I learned about the subject from the 51 interviews I conducted for this book. The model of the advisory process that I give is a guide to scientific advising, not a set of necessary conditions.

In the final sections, I reflect on the reputation of a scientific advisory service and on the issue of trust and science. I explain why it is important for advisers to be trustworthy, compare trusting scientists and trusting activists, describe how social information cascades lead to polarisation in controversial topics and explain why impartiality is key in science. I also add some thoughts on scientific advisers' preparedness to respond to an emergency.

5.1   FRAMING THE ADVISORY PROJECT

5.1.1   The Identification and Framing Phases

A scientific advisory project begins when a policy-maker asks for advice on a policy issue or problem. I assume for simplicity that the problem involves a new technology. The first and most important decision in preparing scientific advice is determining the project's focus. This is best done by clearly framing the problem with a set of questions and answering them in ways that are of interest to the policy-maker. Well-formulated questions will guide many aspects of the project, from collecting evidence to communicating policy options.

Advisers first familiarise themselves with the problem as the policy-maker conceives it. They then frame the problem as a research question. Ensuring the political impartiality of their advice begins in the framing stage. When the problem is of a political nature, advisers frame the research question apolitically, and they bring to light and eliminate any political or ideological biases they have, which they might otherwise incorporate into the framing. They must frame the research question so that it includes the specific focuses that the policy-maker requested. They must also frame it to cover the interests and concerns of all of the stakeholders and, to avoid bias, the widest range of such perspectives possible. In general, then, the research question is wider than the original problem. If the problem involves a high degree of uncertainty, I recommend that the advising project include a scenario-based foresight investigation, and advisers decide in the framing stage the form that their engagement with stakeholders will take.

So, the framing stage ends with a description of the project's scope, a well-formulated research question and a plan for addressing it. Advisers should also make a projection of the resources that the research will require. All of this can be put in the form of a scoping paper.

5.1.2 Systems Analysis: A Step Towards a Holistic View

After the framing stage comes a systems analysis. In the initial systems analysis, advisers zoom out from the research question to get a holistic overview of it, including the main steps in the research; whether it will require external expertise; the relevant stakeholders and the time frame, which may have to be negotiated with the policy-maker.

In the analysis, advisers first break the research question down into sub-questions. To ensure that they do not overlook any appropriate sub-question, they analyse the research question in accordance with the

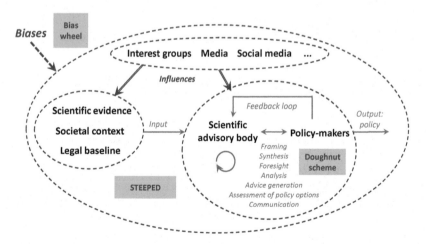

Fig. 5.1 The science-policy ecosystem's components relevant for scientific advisers

STEEPED wheel (Fig. 3.4), which guides the analysis along seven perspectives (social, technological, environmental, economic, political/legal, ethical and demographic). Next, they determine the types and sources of scientific and societal inputs to the research. To determine the societal inputs, advisers conduct a stakeholder analysis in which they identify those who are affected by the problem and will be affected by, or can affect, the policy decision. Using STEEPED ensures that they do not overlook any relevant stakeholders. Finally, advisers determine the legislative texts that they will have to consult. Figure 5.1, a revised version of Fig. 1.2, diagrams the systems analysis.

5.2   Sources of Input

Advisers should draw on a wide range of sources of input. Four types of input can be distinguished:

- Available evidence syntheses;
- Original scientific evidence;
- Stakeholders' views;
- The legislative state of the art.

5.2.1   Sources of Scientific Evidence and Its Synthesis

> Evidence synthesis is the process of bringing together information and knowledge from many and varied sources to inform debates and decisions.

To provide value for the money, advisers should not duplicate work already done. So, determining the inputs to the research begins with an overview of existing work on the research sub-questions, and closely related questions, and an overview of evidence syntheses that fellow advisory services and knowledge centres, such as research agencies, have already provided. Because they are usually well-written and accessible, the syntheses of high-level think tanks can also be useful, but that requires some vigilance. According to Helga Nowotny (Nowotny et al. 2001), it is disputable whether think tanks and management consultants are extensions of traditional knowledge institutions. And due to their nature, they are not always impartial. So, advisers should check a think tank's ideology, purpose and funding before using its evidence synthesis. James G. McGann's annual *Think Tank Index Report* (2018) is a good guide for judging the trustworthiness of specific think tanks. On the condition that scientific advisers check them carefully, I believe that input from think tanks enhances value for the money.

According to interviewees, the syntheses of governmental research agencies are more trustworthy than those of think tanks. A few examples of such research agencies are the European Environmental Agency (EEA), the European Food Safety Authority (EFSA), the Joint Research Centre of the European Commission (JRC), the International Energy Agency (IEA), the European Space Agency (ESA), the US's National Aeronautics and Space Administration (NASA) and the Intergovernmental Panel on Climate Change (IPCC). Such knowledge centres provide advisers transparent, tailored and concise information about the latest scientific evidence and, so, save them time and taxpayers' money. Whatever their sources, though, advisers should always critically examine evidence syntheses, updating them when appropriate, and double-check those produced by other bodies for their quality and impartiality.

The appropriate use of science in policy advising requires scientific advisers to be what Roger Pielke calls "honest brokers". So, their own syntheses should reflect the breadth of scientific opinion. The practice of the Oxford Martin School Restatements ("Oxford Martin Restatements" 2019) is an excellent model for synthesizing evidence. Researchers from various disciplines review the scientific evidence relating to areas of policy concern, including controversial ones, for example, 'The Natural Science Evidence Base on the Effects of Endocrine Disrupting Chemicals on Wildlife' (Stephens et al. 2019) and 'Health Effects of Low-Level Ionizing Radiation' (Elliott et al. 2017); summarise it in a way that is comprehensible to an informed but non-expert reader and introduce the technical literature. They are as impartial as possible, consulting with a very broad community (including researchers, industry, NGOs and government) but writing their reports independently of any stakeholder.

5.2.2 *Some Reflections on the Limits of Science and Evidence*

Science tells us how things work but not how to use that knowledge.

Science is powerful. It has produced the knowledge that allows us to live as we do with medical treatments, telecommunications, computers, fast transportation and the production of energy and food. But science is not sacred. I consider some of its critics' reflections on its limits, for scientists and scientific advisers have to be aware of them. I first explain three limits that I discussed with my interviewees. Next, I discuss some detailed criticisms of the governance of science and of how it is assumed to assure the quality of research. I also explain the concept of Post Normal Science (PNS).

One limit is that since science incorporates assumptions, it can be wrong. So, scientists, and scientific advisers, must be aware of their assumptions, which include their biases. Another limit is that science cannot justify normative conclusions. Since science discovers how the world is, it can inform individuals' opinions and decisions whatever their background knowledge, beliefs or cultural education. But for the same reason, it can come to no conclusions about whether the way the world is is right or wrong, good or bad. A third limit is that science does not tell one how to use the knowledge it discovers. There are good and bad ways to use that knowledge, but we cannot consult science in deciding how to use it.

These decisions are in everyone's hands but especially the hands of policy-makers and their advisers. Since policy-makers cannot decide normative policy issues on the basis of scientific evidence alone, policy advisers do not limit themselves to it; they take stakeholders' opinions, values and preferences into account. In addressing climate change, for instance, one can imagine extreme policies that the public would not accept. Therefore, advisers have to balance the scientific evidence and societal acceptability, and, since policies should be fair to all societal groups, policy-makers must make trade-offs.

In *Scientific Knowledge: Its Social Problems* (Ravetz 1971), Jerome Ravetz criticizes 'scientific objectivity', which he takes to be 'the supposedly value-free character of science' with which one is 'indoctrinated as a part of the implicit background to science education'. Thus, he claims that science students find it almost inconceivable to criticise the objectivity of science. Nevertheless, he asserts, scientists must understand that it is not the case that every scientific problem has just one solution. Furthermore, since science involves funding, reputation, publication and social and cultural concerns, Ravetz considers the possibility that scientists' conclusions cannot be trusted at all. Especially when a science-related problem involves many uncertainties and the risks of relevant policies are high, one cannot assume that the experts know best. Normative debates over value-laden issues, such as nuclear energy, genomics and artificial intelligence, have educated the public about the limits of scientific objectivity. Thus, Ravetz argues that scientific integrity is more important than scientific objectivity.

Who guards the guardians?

In *The No-Nonsense Guide to Science* (Ravetz et al. 2006), Ravetz and his co-authors criticize scientists for the growing crisis in the quality of scientific conclusions and the reliability of its quality-assurance. They explain the crisis in terms of the very success of science, which has resulted in 'the industrialisation of science'. In addressing scientists' responsibility for assuring the quality of their conclusions, they ask, 'Who guards the guardians?' They also argue that science is no longer an independent player. It has a place in the 'extended peer community', which includes society and policy and which employs the 'extended facts' of the society in addressing problems.

In *Science for the Post-Normal Age* (Funtowicz and Ravetz 1993), Ravetz and Funtowicz argue that scientific evidence and expert judgment are an inadequate basis for policy decisions in areas where the facts are uncertain, values are in dispute, the stakes are high and decisions are urgent, as in policy areas pertaining to safety, health and the environment, for example, climate change. So, they develop a role for science to play in such areas that they call "Post-Normal Science" (PNS). PNS concentrates on three aspects of the complex relation between science and policy: the communication of uncertainty, the assessment of quality and the forms of justification. The community includes more than one discipline relevant to a policy issue; so, it provides different lenses through which to consider it. And PNS extends the policy discussion to all of those with a stake in the issue. 25 years after they developed it, PNS applies to today's most urgent policy challenges, to which scientists, consultants and policy professionals have no solutions to offer.

5.2.3 Sources of Influence on Public Opinion

Science is not the only source of solutions to policy problems. In the course of an advisory project, advisers supplement the scientific evidence with two other inputs illustrated in Fig. 5.1, society and interest groups.

Interest groups, e.g., pressure groups, advocacy groups, lobbying groups and civil-society organizations, operate in the business community, government and civil society, and they employ various forms of advocacy to influence public opinion. But they also exert their influence on scientists, policy-makers and scientific advisers (cf. Figs. 1.2 and 5.1).

The latter must pay particular attention to the category of interest groups that Naomi Oreskes and Erik M. Conway call "merchants of doubt". In their book *Merchants of Doubt: How a Handful of Scientists Obscured the Truth on Issues from Tobacco Smoke to Global Warming* (Oreskes and Conway 2010), they describe how merchants of doubt employ propaganda and disinformation to hijack the dissemination of scientific information to the public. The basic strategy that such interest groups employ to prevent policy action is spreading doubt and confusion to 'keep the controversy alive' after a scientific consensus had been reached. Oreskes and Conway describe some remarkable parallels between the denial of climate change and earlier denials about smoking, acid rain and the hole in the ozone layer. In each case, those opposing policy action applied the basic strategy in the same way, namely, they raised doubts in the public's mind by inflating uncertainties in the science, which are inevitable, and exploiting the media's principle of balanced coverage to publicize the 'other side of the story'.

For example, the millions of pages of tobacco industry documents that successful litigation forced into the open revealed that the industry's own scientists had concluded by the early 1960s that smoking causes cancer and nicotine is addictive. But that was not its public position. It argued that there was no conclusive evidence that smoking is unhealthy and, later, none that second-hand smoke is harmful. In a memo in 1969, an industry executive wrote,

> Doubt is our product... It is also the means of establishing a controversy. ... If in our pro-cigarette efforts we stick to well documented fact, we can dominate a controversy and operate with the confidence of justifiable self-interest. (Unknown 1969)

According to Oreskes and Conway, doubt, which drives scientific progress when in the form of healthy scepticism, also makes its conclusions vulnerable to misrepresentation. 'This was the tobacco industry's key insight: that you could use normal scientific uncertainty to undermine the status of actual scientific knowledge'.

It worked to delay action in the three historical cases Oreskes and Conway describe, sometimes for decades, and it is working again with climate change. The lesson for advisers is to be careful about the amount of attention they give to the 'other side of the story', for too much can magnify the public's unfounded doubts. They can guard against the inappropriate influence of interest groups by carefully checking the impartiality of their sources of information. And they can anticipate policy-makers' doubts by keeping track of the sources of doubt and the contexts in which it arises. It is essential to balance inputs, but they must balance evidence-based and interest-based inputs cautiously.

Another source of enormous influence on public opinion is the media, for it often sets the public's agenda by deciding what issues and events to cover and how much coverage to give them. All of the actors in the science-policy ecosystem are subject to the media's influence.

5.2.4   *Legislative Input*

The advisory project's inputs include an overview of institutional memory (Chapter 1, Figs. 1.2 and 5.1), which advisers employ in the analysis of policy options and the design of roadmaps to possible futures. The research sub-questions formulated in the scoping report at the end of the framing phase are a good basis for assembling relevant legislative texts.

5.3   FORESIGHT: ADVISING ON THE BASIS OF MORE THAN SCIENTIFIC EVIDENCE

In the foresight phase, advisers collect information on the societal views of the policy problem, on the basis of which they will contextualize the scientific evidence into evidence-based, socially acceptable policy options. Again, I assume that the problem involves a new technology.

5.3.1   *Preparing a Foresight Brainstorming Session*

As part of the outward systems analysis, advisers generate a list of stakeholder groups. At the start of the foresight phase, they select expert representatives of these stakeholders and invite them to a foresight meeting for brainstorming about the possible impacts of the technology and the policy for it, in which they will enumerate the concerns of the societal groups they represent. Advisers should invite participants with sufficiently varied backgrounds to ensure an interdisciplinary investigation. Ideally, the brainstorming group, including advisers, policy-makers, experts and facilitators, does not exceed 25 individuals.

A wide variety of facilitation techniques are available to collect participants' views. "What if" questions are a powerful tool for thinking about the possible effects of a new technology, and I recommend their use. Ravetz also advises systematically posing "what if" questions in conversations on science and its applications to policy problems. "What if" also expresses the Precautionary Principle, which applies to policy actions on issues involving uncertainty and which is increasingly important in policy for the environment and technologies that involve many uncertainties (e.g., genetic engineering) or are socially disruptive (e.g., robotics and artificial intelligence). "What if" questions prevent advisers from formulating on policy options for techno-scientific issues too hastily.

5.3.2   Foresight: Envisioning Possible Impacts

As part of preparing for the foresight meeting, advisers, perhaps with the help of external technical experts, prepare a presentation for participants that explains the research question and accessibly summarize the scientific evidence. They may also conduct a preparatory STEEPED analysis of the technology to generate initial concerns about and possible policies for it and on their basis prepare some "what if" questions to guide the session. According to my experience, combining "what if" questions with STEEPED quickly deepens the discussion of impacts, especially unintended and soft impacts and those 10 years and more in the future.

After advisers give their presentation and answer the audience's questions about it, all of the participants brainstorm about the technology's possible impacts (see Sect. 3.2). There is no need for participants to reach any consensus on their concerns, which can cover the range from the very likely to the very implausible.

5.3.3   Foresight Widens Spatial and Temporal Perspectives

The aim of scientific foresight is to collect information on society's hopes and fears about the technology's possible impacts. According to *The Limits of Growth* (Robinson et al. 1973), a Report to the Club of Rome in 1973, people focus primarily on short-term consequences in their vicinity. As Fig. 5.2 (inspired by the Report's Figure 1) illustrates, brainstorming on

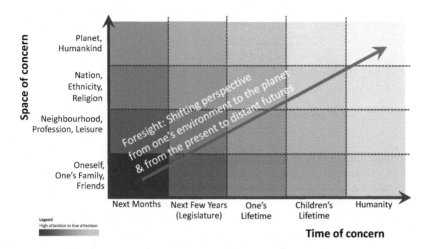

Fig. 5.2 Foresight shifting participants' concerns to wider times and spaces

"what if" questions in the foresight meeting draws participants' attention to a broader range of possible effects in wider environments and longer time frames. By incorporating participants' broadened perspectives on the technology's impacts, advisers' scientific advice will be that much more future-proof.

5.3.4 Foresight Reveals the Societal Context

The outcome of this part of the foresight phase is a list of societal concerns. Advisers then propose explorative scenarios for participants to investigate those concerns in more detail. These investigations uncover key societal issues that the policy must address. For example, STOA's foresight investigation of the ethics of robotics (Chapter 3) revealed that liability for accidents with self-driving cars was a key societal concern, and that discovery led the European Parliament to call for EU-wide liability rules for robots and artificial intelligence. In this way, advisers gather insights into society's collective policy preferences and aversions, and they take those into consideration in their formulation and assessment of policy options.

In investigating explorative scenarios, participants can also envision new areas in which to apply a policy. For example, STOA's foresight study 'Assistive Technologies for People with Disabilities' (Boucher 2018) included

explorative scenarios about people without disabilities using assistive technologies, and exploring them revealed possible applications of these technologies in such people's professional and personal lives, for example, in
communication.

5.4   Development and Assessment of Policy Options

Though other experts involved in the advising project may suggest policy options on the basis of the scientific evidence, the responsibility for
formulating the policy options that constitute the advice to policy-makers
belongs entirely to the scientific advisers. The UK's Government Office
for Science addressed the need to separate these roles in its 'Code of Practice for Scientific Advisory Committees' (Government Office for Science
2011).

5.4.1   Formulation of Policy Options

After the foresight group has explored the futures to which a technology
might lead, advisers select a set of diverse scenarios and with them in mind
formulate a range of policy options that reflect what they learned in the
foresight phase. So, they articulate the policy options on the basis of a
realistic view of the futures that stakeholders find desirable and undesirable.

Consider, for example, the scenario of cameras in the workplace that recognize employees' faces and track their emotions on the basis of their facial
expressions. Advisers formulate different sets of regulations that address the
concerns that the technology raised in the foresight session, for example,
securing employees' privacy and protecting them against discrimination.

5.4.2   Roadmaps to the Future: Legal Backcasting

Once they have formulated a set of policy options for each of the selected
futures, advisers design roadmaps to, and away from, those futures that
start from the current legal framework. This is the legal backcasting phase.

5.4.3 Assessing Cross-Policy Impacts

In the legal backcasting phase, advisers also assess policy options for their impacts on existing policies. Without this assessment, their advice to policy-makers can lead to policy decisions that are later regretted and have to be revised, as happened with the biofuel policy (Chapter 4). Cross-policy assessment also makes policy-makers aware of any blind spots they may have.

5.5   COMMUNICATING THE SCIENTIFIC ADVICE

According to several interviewees, the ideal for communicating scientific information to policy-makers is the honest broker.

5.5.1 The Stages of Attention

If they are to communicate their advice successfully, advisers must first get policy-makers' unprejudiced attention. That is harder to do than ever before, for nowadays getting the attention of one's audience includes getting its digital attention, but with all of the new media developed in the last decades, there has never been stiffer competition for audiences' digital attention. In *Captivology: The Science of Capturing People's Attention* (Parr 2016), Ben Parr explains the consecutive stages of attention. The first stage, immediate attention, is a fast and unconscious reaction to a stimulus, for instance, a gunshot. The second stage is short attention, in which one chooses to pay attention to something in one's environment, as when one listens to a speaker or reads a newspaper article. The third stage, long attention, is manifest in one's sustained interest in a subject, like a fan's interest in a celebrity. Immediate attention is a form of Daniel Kahneman's fast thinking (Kahneman 2012) and Theo Compernolle's reflex brain (Compernolle 2014); long attention involves Kahneman's slow thinking and Compernolle's reflecting brain (see Sect. 2.1). Advisers want policy-makers' long attention, their long-term interest in their advice and the evidence justifying it.

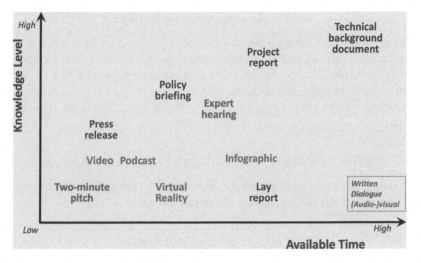

Fig. 5.3   Communication formats for scientific advice

5.5.2   Formats for Communicating Scientific Advice

Scientific advisers should make their advice clear and applicable. As I learned from my interviewees, there is no single way to do this, for different policy-makers are differently invested in different policy issues, and their technical and scientific background knowledge varies. Consequently, the appropriate format for communicating the advice to policy-makers with diverse involvement in the policy issue varies from a two-minute pitch to a detailed technical report that includes all of the evidence. Communication formats include written communication as well as expert hearings, podcasts and videos, infographics and—why not—potentially also Virtual Reality. Figure 5.3 summarizes communication formats in terms of presentation and attention time and audience expertise.

5.5.3   Framing the Evidence

In general, people want information they can understand. In the chapter 'Using Frames to Make Scientific Communication More Effective' of the *Oxford Handbook of the Science of Science Communication* (Druckman and Lupia 2017), James N. Druckman and Arthur Lupia explore the impact of frames on scientific communication. They state:

People can pay attention to only a very small amount of information at one time. For scientists who seek to convey insights assembled from studies of complex phenomena, the reality of limited capacity forces them to make choices about how to convey what they know.

So, scientific communicators must decide on the key message to convey and what to leave for later. Framing involves focusing the audience's attention on certain information by contextualizing it in a relevant field of meaning. Choosing the right frame is the key to conveying scientific information effectively. So, one must make choices about what and on which technical level to communicate. This constitutes a serious challenge for scientific advisers. Several interviewees thought that advisers complicate their communication by not carefully selecting what they most want to convey and not formulating it at the appropriate level. Advisers must frame their advice carefully since the frame both enables the audience to understand the communicator and allows the communicator to manipulate the audience.

Three examples illustrate how appropriate framing can capture an audience's short attention and focus it on scientific information by making it relevant. First, imagine publishing a report on the MMR vaccine against measles, mumps and rubella. If you publish the report just before a holiday during which many people travel, you can quickly get your audience's attention by highlighting the information that unvaccinated international travellers are at risk of contracting measles and bringing the disease back home.

Next, imagine speaking about waste management and the circular economy. Saying that the EU produces about 2.5 billon tons of waste annually may frame the information too abstractly to get your audience's attention. However, in his short video about the circular economy (European Parliamentary Research Service 2018), Didier Bourguignon, my colleague at the European Parliamentary Research Service, framed his information more powerfully by saying, 'Altogether, each one of us in the European Union generates around 13 kg of waste per day.' Hearing that may well make you more attentive to what comes next as you may find that figure unbelievable until it is explained. Bourguignon's framing is an example of what Ben Parr calls a "disruption trigger", i.e., it upsets people's expectations, which causes them to pay closer attention. We used a similar disruption trigger to frame information in the opening of a video that we produced for the European Parliament on the ecological footprint of food: 'Did you know it takes around 2,500 hundred litres of water to produce a single hamburger?' (STOA 2013).

Finally, in speaking about climate change, rather than explaining the effect of a 2°–4° increase in air temperature on the sea level in terms of the number of centimetres the sea may rise, you can more powerfully frame the information with a map depicting the areas that would be at risk of flooding, for these areas may be of personal interest to the audience.

5.5.4   Communicating Uncertainty

According to several interviewees, the ideal for communicating scientific information to policy-makers is the honest broker.

One way that interviewees recommend for advisers to earn policy-makers' trust is to communicate their uncertainties. However, policy-makers, and many others, find it difficult to cope with uncertainty and probability. Most of the interviewees assume that most non-scientists lack sufficient statistical literacy to understand probabilities. And it is not easy to acquire. One likened instructing politicians in enough of the basics of statistics to make them comfortable with probability to teaching someone Russian in three days. Therefore, scientific advisers have to find ways to communicate uncertainty that lay people can understand.

5.5.5   Reflections on Perceptions of Scientific Evidence

Many of the policy areas in which science is relevant are the subjects of persistent controversy, for instance, genetically modified food, vaccination, climate change and nuclear energy. In 'Sources of Ordinary Science Knowledge and Extraordinary Science Ignorance' (Kahan 2017), Dan Kahan investigates problems in communicating scientific information arising from the persistence of deep public divisions on the relevance of scientific evidence to policy in such areas. Among the problems are that scientists presume that the public is irrational (but the fact that people are more likely to believe the opinions of their peers than they are to accept scientific conclusions does not necessarily mean that they are irrational), scientists' belief that the public tends to criticize them as obscure and partisan, scientists' depiction of the public's worries over controversial science-related issues as expressions of their anti-science sensibilities and scientists' assumption that the public is being manipulated.

Interviewees agreed with Kahan about these problems, particularly that citizens' judgements about the accuracy of evidence are strongly influenced by their anxiety over issues like vaccines and food safety and that interest groups, social media and some NGOs have too much influence in some policy areas. They also believed that the public's distrust of science, or its greater trust in information it receives from the traditional and social media, is probably due to its insufficient scientific knowledge.

5.6   THE SCIENTIFIC ADVISORY PROCESS: A MODEL

In this section, I provide a summary framework for preparing and delivering scientific advice. Figure 5.4 depicts one model of, not necessary conditions for, the course of a scientific advisory project. Advisers can adapt the model as the complexity and urgency of the policy problem and the resources available demand. Combining a systems analysis of the issue with bias checks, multi-disciplinary STEEPED explorations, foresight investigations with multiple stakeholders, cross-policy impact analyses and quality control of the evidence allows for much creativity.

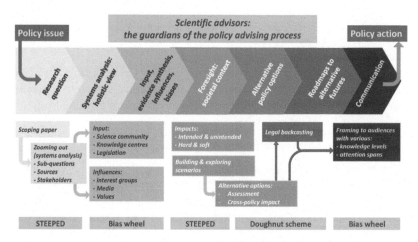

Fig. 5.4   Steps and tools in a typical foresight-based scientific advisory project

5.6.1   Project Definition: Scoping

In the scoping phase, advisers re-examine their research question, analysing its complexity and relevance to the policy problem. They may broaden the scope of the research question to make it relevant to more policy areas. They also consider resource constraints (staff, expertise, budget) and the time frame. They compile the results in a scoping paper.

5.6.2   Systems Analysis in Practice

In the systems analysis, they zoom out to get the broad picture of the problem and identify the relevant sources of input, stakeholders, influences and related policies. A systems analysis is not complicated; it is a matter of common sense. The STEEPED wheel and the following questions guide the systems analysis:

- Who?
- What?
- Where?
- When?
- Why?
- How?

for which one can use the mnemonic 'five Whiskeys and a Hangover'. The first three matter for the scoping paper. The second three are useful in formulating policy options and developing roadmaps to possible futures.

5.6.3   Collection and Synthesis of Input

Advisers first collect and assess available evidence syntheses and update them if needed. They then gather other appropriate evidence and synthesize the total scientific input. They investigate other influences in the ecosystem, e.g., the opinion statements of interest groups. Finally, they list the available legislation, which will be the baseline for their legal backcastings.

5.6.4   Foresight: The Societal Context

Advisers gather evidence of the problem's societal context in a foresight intervention of all types of impact with experts and a wide range of stakeholders. A foresight intervention does not provide empirical societal evidence unless it includes scientific methods, for instance, surveys. If the project is to include a scientific study of societal views, it should be included in the scoping paper.

On the basis on the synthesis of the scientific evidence, stakeholders and technical experts envision the technology's possible (intended and unintended, hard and soft) impacts. Advisers organize these into a set of explorative scenarios, including extreme ones, describing desired as well as disruptive futures.

5.6.5   Analysing Alternatives for Anticipating the Future

Advisers select scenarios and devise roadmaps to the futures they describe. Their baselines are the available legislation. The question 'How?' guides the drawing of roadmaps.

5.6.6   Communicating the Advice

Advisers communicate their advice in a range of formats, depending on the audience's investment in the issue and background knowledge. They communicate it as honest brokers to the policy-makers who asked for it in a policy briefing that includes their policy options, the evidence supporting them, their cross-policy assessments and the roadmaps to the selected possible futures covering the legal, ethical and socio-economic steps to reaching some and avoiding others. Policy-makers use the backcastings to devise concrete policies for arriving at and avoiding those futures. However, advisers do not represent these futures as desirable or undesirable. That is for the policy-makers to decide.

Advisers follow up on the adequacy of their advice via feedback loops with policy-makers. If required, they supply more details or conduct a follow-up study.

The scientific advisers are responsible for the entire process from the request for advice to the communication of it, and they should document the steps.

5.7   An Advisory Service's Reputation

It is important for an advisory service's credibility that it follow transparent procedures. And its advisers must have good reputations if it wants policy-makers and others to be interested in its advice. In *Captivology* (Parr 2016), Ben Parr calls this the "reputation trigger".

A parliamentary research service acquires a good reputation by delivering transparently produced, politically neutral, scientifically objective and well-informed analyses that members of parliament and their staff, the wider government and policy communities can understand. It should also communicate probabilities and uncertainties clearly. Interviewees recommended that scientific advisory services cultivate a brand, and a prerequisite of branding is thorough quality assurance.

5.7.1   Impartiality

To ensure a scientific advisory service's political impartiality, policy-makers should understand the procedures it follows. Advisers may consult policy-makers when preparing the project's scoping paper, but they should not consult them during the collection of evidence. As stakeholders, policy-makers are involved in the foresight phase, but they have no further involvement until the communication phase.

5.7.2   A Multidisciplinary Advisory Team

To ensure that its advice is of the highest quality, an advisory team should be sufficiently multidisciplinary to engage in interdisciplinary discussions. I recommend that it also include advisers of different ages so that senior members guide younger ones and younger ones contribute fresh ideas. A sceptically minded team member is useful for quality control of a study's design and its intermediate and final conclusions. And though I do not know of any scientific advisory service that employs one, a psychologist would be useful on the team, for instance, in planning communications.

Most advisory services do not employ a sufficiently interdisciplinary staff of researchers to be able to conduct all of its studies in-house. However, many have transparent and reliable procedures for outsourcing their studies. Outside experts should also be sufficiently interdisciplinary and have different geographical and cultural backgrounds. External researchers may formulate draft policy options, but responsibility for the final version, which will be based on the contractors' evidence, rests with the advisory service.

5.7.3   Quality Assurance

Quality control is crucial for policy-makers to trust the advice they receive from scientific advisers. More generally, an advisory service should have clear guidelines for its sources of evidence, how it investigates them, how it infers conclusions and so on. And its quality control procedures should include documenting that they were followed. Scientific advisory services should adopt standardized methods, which are clear to policy-makers, as in the scheme I outlined in the previous section.

Possible quality control procedures include advisers' systems analysis and their investigation of the problem from all perspectives by the use of STEEPED (Figs. 3.3 and 3.4); their assessment of the impact of policy options on other policies, using the doughnut (Fig. 4.2); and the investigation of possible biases throughout the science-policy ecosystem, using the bias-check wheel (Fig. 2.1). Quality control must also cover the clarity and precision of reports' language and the consistency of their style. Finally, it should cover timeliness. The reports of reputable advisory services draw many outside readers, which interviewees take as indicating the quality of their communications.

In '2017 Global Go to Think Tank Index Report' (McGann 2018), James G. McGann provides a detailed list of quality criteria for think tanks, many of which apply to advisory services. Some of these are:

1. The quality and commitment of its leadership, including the management of its mission and projects, and the mobilisation of the resources necessary to fulfil the mission and monitor quality, independence and impact;
2. The quality and reputation of its staff and of the independent research it produces;
3. The quality, number and reach of its publications;
4. Its reputation with policy-makers;
5. Access to key institutions, that is, the ability to connect with key audiences, such as elected and appointed government officials, civil society, traditional and new media and academia;

6. The ability to convene key policy actors and develop effective networks and partnerships with other knowledge centres (e.g., think tanks and research agencies);
7. The effective transmission of its products to policy-makers and the policy community and their utilization of them;
8. Its website and digital presence and its ability to use electronic, print and new media to communicate research to key audiences, including policy-makers, journalists and the public.

5.7.4   Value for Money

Interviewees commented on the balance between quality and expenditure of financial, human and time resources. Finding this balance requires carefully considering the project's purpose and constraints. Value for the money is part of the balance. Taxpayers finance most scientific advice. Whether an increase in quality is worth the added expense should be decided one case at a time, for some issues are more relevant to policy and society than others.

5.8   Science and Trust

Doubts about the validity of scientific evidence can undermine citizens' confidence in science and evidence-based policy, and without trust in science one does not consider scientific evidence with an open and critical mind. So, I end the book with some reflections on trust and science, namely, the importance of scientists' trustworthiness, trusting scientists versus trusting activists, how social media polarize people's opinions on controversial subjects and the importance of impartiality.

5.8.1   Trust in Science and the Trustworthiness of Scientists

The contemporary controversy over the applicability of scientific evidence to policy may make it seem as if the public has lost its trust in science and scientists. However, opinion polls show that this is not the case. The 'Veracity Index 2018' (Skinner and Clemence 2018), published by the global market research firm IPSOS, reveals that scientists are among the professionals most trusted in the United Kingdom to tell the truth. The most trusted are nurses (96%), followed by doctors (92%), teachers (89%), professors (86%) and scientists (85%). The least trusted professionals are advertising executives (16%), the only professionals the British trust less than politicians (19%), government ministers (22%) and journalists (26%). However, surveys in 2018 by the Pew Research Center (Funk and Kennedy 2019) and other polling organizations show wide public disagreement in the United States over scientific issues like climate change and genetically modified food.

What make scientists, and scientific advisers, trustworthy? In 'A Question Of Trust' (O'Neill 2002), the philosopher Onora O'Neill argues that being competent in a certain matter, and being honest all the time, makes a person trustworthy in that matter. According to O'Neill and several interviewees, what really matters for scientists and scientific advisors is not whether they are trusted but whether they are trustworthy. There are both simple and complicated systems of accountability that institutions can abide by, for instance, following transparent procedures and documenting them with checklists, that will make them trustworthy. However, accountability systems risk having the opposite effect, for they can distract scientists and advisers from their core tasks.

In several interviews, I focused on scientific advisers' trustworthiness in communicating uncertain evidence. Interviewees agreed that they should avoid seeming overconfident. According to one, scientists who ignore uncertainties are deeply untrustworthy and should not be in positions of authority.

5.8.2 Trusting Scientists Versus Trusting NGOs

Interviewees believed that the public trusts NGOs, especially activist groups, more than scientists and that as a result big NGOs, like Greenpeace and the World Wildlife Fund, are very powerful. According to one, the reason for the greater trust is that the public thinks of NGOs as David in the fight with Goliath: Everyone likes David; no one likes Goliath. They believed that the public does trust scientists' claims as long as trusted NGOs do not criticise them, but when they do, then scientists have almost no chance of being believed. Especially with controversial subjects, worried citizens find the claims of well-known NGOs more trustworthy than those of scientists, particularly when they are members. People think of trusted NGOs as part of their in-group, in part because they communicate in ways they understand. NGOs communicate at the knowledge level of their members; so, they describe the scientific evidence to the public at its level. However, interviewees believed that the trust that people invest in

NGOs that evaluate scientific evidence does not depend on the evidence evaluated; it depends on their belief that the organization shares their values. Several interviewees expressed frustration over trusted NGOs having criticized their research results, as they believed that this erodes the public's trust in science. They were also frustrated that NGOs that claim to base their positions on scientific evidence usually will not engage in discussion with scientists. Scientists among the interviewees thought that NGOs do not always acknowledge the full range of evidence. And most interviewees thought that their business model made powerful NGOs intrinsically biased, and they stressed that the missions of NGOs and the scientific community are different, even when they deal with the same matters.

In 'Science and NGO Practice: Facts and Figures' (Makri 2013), Anita Makri confirms interviewees' belief that scientists and NGOs have little chance of interacting, for, as she explains, some NGOs are critics of science and technology or watchdogs over innovations like genetic modification, synthetic biology and nuclear power. Makri's analysis of their different practices shows that, though NGOs may accept the validity of scientific methods, their work often incorporates political and social interests, which most scientists, who also have such interests, separate from their work. Interviewees agreed with her conclusion, saying that NGOs' claims about evidence tend to be prejudiced by their political and social interests.

The general public is only modestly literate about science. (This is the knowledge bias I described in Chapter 1.) And they do not think in the ways that scientists do. They judge risks on the basis of intuition and emotion. Therefore, the public tends to overestimate the risks of emotionally charged dangers, such as terrorist attacks. Non-scientists are also more likely to believe the opinions of their peers, which can trigger polarization. It is also for these reasons, in addition to those that interviewees gave, that the public trusts what NGOs say about the scientific evidence relevant to policy more than what scientists say.

Citizens' relative mistrust of science compared to NGOs is different in nature from their distrust of scientists who work for controversial industries, for they believe that such scientists cannot be trusted at all because they are motivated only by financial gain and paid by their industries to say what they do.

5.8.3 *Social Information Cascades Cause Polarisation*

Policy professionals in the digital era must understand how social media influence the ways that individuals inform themselves and form their opinions. Almost every interviewee pointed to social media as a major influence on the public's beliefs about the science behind policy-making, and some mentioned the social cascades that disrupt the dissemination of accurate and unbiased information to the public.

Behavioural psychologists and behavioural economists study information cascades, in which individuals observe the decisions or opinions of others and form their own opinions on that basis, rather than consulting the facts. Social cascades are information cascades that occur on social media. In *#Republic* (2017), Cass Sunstein explains that social cascades, which are often hard, and sometimes impossible, to predict, organise public opinion on complicated and controversial issues (such as climate change, genetically modified food and vaccination). The more complicated or controversial an issue, the more tempting it is to select information on the basis of hash tags (#), and, so, the easier it is for someone to spread an opinion, including falsehoods, to hundreds, thousands or even millions with the press of a button. This way of gathering information puts people into echo chambers or information cocoons.

As Sunstein explains, social cascades can polarise the public on scientific issues, and the anchor, confirmation, knowledge, attention and in-group biases (Chapter 2) can reinforce the polarisation. In this way, people's disagreements and their confidence in their views become extreme.

5.8.4 *Impartiality*

Science communicators should be aware of value-laden words, which can twist audiences' interpretations of what they say. And they should avoid crossing the line between reporting on facts and advocating policy if they do not want to compromise their trustworthiness. Scientists should, as a general rule, stick to the evidence and stay away from recommending policy.

5.9 Scientific Advice in Responding to an Emergency

In this last section, I add some thoughts on scientific advisers' preparedness to respond to an emergency. As interviewees explained, thorough scientific advice takes time to prepare; so, it is not always ready when it is needed.

Therefore, advisers must be prepared to present provisional conclusions on different time scales for different needs. For example, policy-makers sometimes need scientific advice to respond to an emergency, like a natural disaster, a nuclear incident, an epidemic, a computer calamity or an economic crisis. They must then make decisions quickly; however, they must base their decisions on evidence.

In anticipation of crises, I recommend that scientific advisers establish procedures for providing emergency advice. They should include a prompt crisis meeting for analysing the problem, identifying and involving the experts needed to address it and making provisions for their immediate analysis and formulation of possible courses of action. The UK's Scientific Advisory Group for Emergencies (SAGE) is an example of such a framework (Bardach and Patashnik 2016; UK Cabinet Office 2012). They should also be transparent. Transparent emergency procedures ensure that policy-makers, politicians, the media and the public trust the use of science and advisers' competence in emergencies.

5.10   CHAPTER SUMMARY AND CONCLUSIONS

To provide impartial, future-proof scientific advice, scientific advisers can combine tools from the kit presented in this book.

A systems analysis broadly outlines their research by zooming out from the policy issue to the wider science-policy ecosystem, including sources of input and influence and stakeholders.

In foresight brainstorming sessions, advisers go beyond the synthesis and analysis of the scientific evidence by contextualizing it in terms of the attitudes of societal stakeholders. By employing STEEPED (Chapter 3), advisers investigate the research question from the widest range of perspectives.

In all of the stages of their project, advisers should be aware of their biases and those of the actors they involve. The bias wheel (Chapter 2) ensures their bias-awareness and, thus, decreases their bias.

Advisers must assess the policy options they formulate for their possible cross-policy impacts (Chapter 4). The doughnut scheme ensures them that they have not overlooked any.

Finally, advisers must communicate their recommendation to policy-makers in ways that recognize their level of engagement and scientific knowledge.

Feedback loops between advisers and policy-makers, established at the start of a project, ensure that advisers have answered the question they were asked and answered it in the way required.

When advisers follow these steps, both policy-makers and society can rely on the resulting scientific advice.

By following the scheme in Fig. 5.4, advisers ensure that policy-makers and society can trust them. This scheme, the bias wheel (Chapter 2), STEEPED (Chapter 3) and the doughnut (Chapter 4) constitute the framework for producing responsible scientific policy advice.

References

Bardach, Eugene, and Eric M. Patashnik. 2016. *A Practical Guide for Policy Analysis: The Eightfold Path to More Effective Problem Solving.* 5th ed. Los Angeles: Sage.

Boucher, Philip. 2018. *Assistive Technologies for People with Disabilities.* Brussels: STOA—European Parliamentary Research Service.

Compernolle, Theo. 2014. *Brain Chains: Discover Your Brain and Unleash Its Full Potential in a Hyperconnected Multitasking World.* Brussels: Compublications.

Druckman, James N., and Arthur Lupia. 2017. "Using Frames to Make Scientific Communication More Effective." In *The Oxford Handbook on the Science of Science Communication,* edited by Kathleen Hall Jamieson, Dan M. Kahan, and Dietram Scheufele. New York: Oxford University Press.

Elliott, Alex, Angela McLean, Charles Godfray, Colin Muirhead, David Mackay, Dudley Goodhead, Elisabeth Cardis, et al. 2017. "'Oxford Martin Restatement 5': A Restatement of the Natural Science Evidence Base Concerning the Health Effects of Low-Level Ionizing Radiation." Oxford Martin School. https://www.oxfordmartin.ox.ac.uk/publications/view/2583. Accessed January 20, 2019.

European Parliamentary Research Service. 2018. "Circular Economy." YouTube Video. https://www.youtube.com/watch?v=u7AgYY6ui54.

Funk, Cary, and Brian Kennedy. 2019. "Public Confidence in Scientists Has Remained Stable for Decades." https://www.pewresearch.org/fact-tank/2019/03/22/public-confidence-in-scientists-has-remained-stable-for-decades/. Accessed March 22, 2019.

Funtowicz, Silvio O., and Jerome R. Ravetz. 1993. "Science for the Post-normal Age." *Futures* 25 (7): 739–755. https://doi.org/10.1016/0016-3287(93)90022-l.

Government Office for Science. 2011. *Code of Practice for Scientific Advisory Committees.* London: UK Government Office for Science. https://assets.publishing.

service.gov.uk/government/uploads/system/uploads/attachment_data/file/ 278498/11-1382-code-of-practice-scientific-advisory-committees.pdf.

Kahan, Dan M. 2017. "On the Sources of Ordinary Science Knowledge and Extraordinary Science Ignorance." In *The Oxford Handbook on the Science of Science Communication*, edited by Kathleen Hall Jamieson, Dan M. Kahan, and Dietram Scheufele, 35–49. New York: Oxford University Press.

Kahneman, Daniel. 2012. *Thinking, Fast and Slow*. London: Penguin.

Makri, Anita 2013. "Science and NGO Practice: Facts and Figures." *Sci Dev Net*. https://www.scidev.net/global/capacity-building/feature/science-and-ngo-practice-facts-and-figures.html. Accessed January 21, 2019.

McGann, James G. 2018. *2017 Global Go to Think Tank Index Report: Vol. 13, TTCSP Global Go To Think Tank Index Reports*. https://repository.upenn.edu/ cgi/viewcontent.cgi?article=1012&context=think_tanks.

Nowotny, Helga, Peter Scott, and Michael Gibbons. 2001. *Re-thinking Science: Knowledge and the Public in an Age of Uncertainty*. Cambridge: Polity Press.

O'Neill, Onora. 2002. *A Question of Trust*. Cambridge: Cambridge University Press.

Oreskes, Naomi, and Erik M. Conway. 2010. *Merchants of Doubt: How a Handful of Scientists Obscured the Truth on Issues from Tobacco Smoke to Global Warming*. New York: Bloomsbury Press.

Oxford Martin School. "Oxford Martin Restatements." https://www. oxfordmartin.ox.ac.uk/policy/restatements/. Accessed January 21, 2019.

Parr, Ben. 2016. *Captivology: The Science of Capturing People's Attention*. New York: HarperOne.

Ravetz, Jerome R. 1971. *Scientific Knowledge and Its Social Problems*. New York: Oxford University Press.

Ravetz, Jerome R., Andrea Saltelli, Silvio Funtowicz, Mario Giampietro, Roger Strand, Ângela Guimarães Pereira, Jeroen van der Sluijs, and Alice Benessia. 2006. *The No-Nonsense Guide to Science*. Oxford: New Internationalist.

Robinson, Warren, Donella H. Meadows, Dennis L. Meadows, Jergen Randers, and William W. Behrens. 1973. *The Limits to Growth: A Report for the Club of Rome's Project on the Predicament of Mankind*. New York: Universe.

Skinner, Gideon, and Michael Clemence. 2018. "Advertising Execs Rank Below Politicians as Britain's Least-Trusted Profession." *Ipsos MORI*. https:// www.ipsos.com/ipsos-mori/en-uk/advertising-execs-rank-below-politicians-britains-least-trusted-profession.

Stephens, Andrea, Andrew Johnson, Angela McLean, Charles Godfray, Charles Tyler, John Sumpter, Paul Jepson, Peter Matthiessen, and Susan Jobling. 2019. "Oxford Martin Restatement 6: A Restatement of the Natural Science Evidence Base on the Effects of Endocrine Disrupting Chemicals on Wildlife." Oxford Martin School. https://www.oxfordmartin.ox.ac.uk/ publications/view/2834.

STOA. 2013. "Food Eco-Foot Print." Edited by Science and Technology Options Assessment: STOA.
Sunstein, Cass R. 2017. *#Republic: Divided Democracy in the Age of Social Media.* Princeton: Princeton University Press.
UK Cabinet Office. 2012. "A Strategic Framework for the Scientific Advisory Group for Emergencies (Sage)." Edited by UK Cabinet Office.
Unknown. 1969. "Smoking and Health Proposal—Tobacco Industry Influence in Public Policy." In *Minnesota Documents,* edited by Brown & Williamson Records.

Conclusion: Scientific Policy Advice Beyond the Evidence

This book offers a concept for scientific advice that bases policy advice on more than scientific evidence by taking into account policies' potential effects on society and the environment. It can be called "Responsible Scientific Advice" (RSA) because of the features that it shares with Responsible Research and Innovation (RRI), which Jack Stilgoe, Richard Owen and Phil Macnaghten have described (Owen et al. 2012; Stilgoe et al. 2013). The book also offers a practical toolkit for scientific policy advisers to anticipate possible future developments in addressing policy issues. These tools allow advisers to balance scientific evidence and other inputs responsibly.

Responsible Scientific Advice (RSA)

RSA is a framework for producing ethically acceptable advice for sustainable policy formulated in the policy's social context and for communicating it to policy-makers in a format is sensitive to their level of scientific knowledge and the amount of time they have to understand it. RSA's basic elements are bias-awareness, multi-perspectival foresight procedures involving a wide range of stakeholders, systems analysis and feedback loops between advisers and policy-makers. RSA is:

1. **Evidence-based:** it takes evidence to be the basis of all scientific advice;

© The Editor(s) (if applicable) and The Author(s), under exclusive license to Springer Nature Switzerland AG, 2020
L. Van Woensel, *A Bias Radar for Responsible Policy-Making*,
St Antony's Series, https://doi.org/10.1007/978-3-030-32126-0

2. **Holistic:** it employs a simple systems analysis to consider the full science-policy ecosystem;
3. **Reflective:** it reveals biases and addresses policy issues from all perspectives;
4. **Inclusive:** it uses a participatory foresight procedure to incorporate the views of the range of stakeholders who are affected by and can affect the policy issue;
5. **Anticipatory:** it investigates a policy's intended effects and the unintended future impacts that are possible, and it assesses its possible cross-policy impacts.
6. **Responsive:** it has a feedback loop between advisers and policy-makers through which advisers make sure, at the start of a project, that they understand the policy problem as policy-makers do and, at the end, that their recommendation meets policy-makers' needs.

A Practical Toolkit for Scientific Policy Advisers

This book's practical toolkit includes:

- A description of the science-policy ecosystem and a list of questions that guide the systems analysis of a policy issue;
- The bias-wheel, for identifying the biases that can arise throughout the scientific advisory process and the science-policy ecosystem; as awareness of bias enhances impartiality, this tool enhances the quality of policy advice;
- The comprehensive STEEPED scheme, which provides a systematic view of the policy issue, plays a central role in foresight practices and allows advisers to enlarge spatial and temporal perspectives, frame policy advice in the broad societal context of its stakeholders and analyse a policy's intended and unintended and hard and soft impacts;
- A framework for identifying existing policies that may conflict with advisers' policy options and the doughnut scheme for assessing such possible cross-policy impacts;
- A summary of the framework of the scientific advisory process of the steps and tools in a typical foresight-based advisory project.

In summary, the book explains that advisers are responsible for the integrity of the scientific advisory process, and it offers them tools to carry out that responsibility by ensuring an awareness of their own and other players' biases and an appropriate balance between scientific evidence and other societal inputs.

REFERENCES

Owen, Richard, Phil Macnaghten, and Jack Stilgoe. 2012. "Responsible Research and Innovation: From Science in Society to Science for Society, with Society." *Science and Public Policy* 39 (6): 751–760. https://doi.org/10.1093/scipol/scs093.

Stilgoe, J., R. Owen, and P. Macnaghten. 2013. "Developing a Framework for Responsible Innovation." *Research Policy* 42 (9): 1568–1580. https://doi.org/10.1016/j.respol.2013.05.008.

Appendix A: Interviewees[1]

1. Dr. Renuka Bahde, Executive Secretary, European Polar Board, The Hague, The Netherlands.
2. Dr. Rob Bellamy, James Martin Research Fellow, Institute for Science, Innovation and Society at the University of Oxford, UK.
3. Didier Bourguignon, Policy Analyst, European Parliamentary Research Service, European Parliament.
4. Dr. Hans Bruyninckx, Executive Director, European Environment Agency.
5. Dr. Kerstin Cuhls, Project Officer for Foresight, Fraunhofer Institute for Systems and Innovation Research ISI, Germany.
6. Dr. Hubert Deluyker, Former Director of the Science Strategy and Coordination Directorate, European Food Safety Authority (EFSA), European Union.
7. Mady Delvaux, Member of the European Parliament, Member of the Panel for the Future of Science and Technology (STOA), European Parliament.
8. Dr. Robert Doubleday, Executive Director, Centre for Science and Policy, Cambridge, UK.
9. Prof. Dr Pearl Dykstra, Professor of Sociology at the Erasmus University Rotterdam; Member of the High-Level Group of Scientists advising the European Commission (SAM), European Commission.

[1] Data at the moment of the interviews.

© The Editor(s) (if applicable) and The Author(s), under exclusive license to Springer Nature Switzerland AG, 2020
L. Van Woensel, *A Bias Radar for Responsible Policy-Making*,
St Antony's Series, https://doi.org/10.1007/978-3-030-32126-0

10. Dr. Alexandra Freeman, Executive Director, Winton Centre for Risk and Evidence Communication, University of Cambridge, UK.
11. Julie Girling, Member of the European Parliament.
12. Prof. Dame Anne Glover, Former Chief Scientific Adviser to the President of the European Commission; member of the Principal's senior advisory team at the University of Strathclyde, UK.
13. Prof. Sir Charles Godfray, Director, Oxford Martin School, University of Oxford, UK.
14. Sharaelle Grzesiak, Foresight Analyst, U.S. Government Accountability Office (GAO), Washington, DC, USA.
15. Wolfgang Hiller, Director of Impact Assessment and European Added Value, European Parliamentary Research Service, European Parliament.
16. James Hynard, Policy Officer for Global Policy, Wellcome Trust, London, UK.
17. Dr. Ana Jakil-Holzer, Deputy Chief of Cabinet, Office of the Government Spokesperson, Austria; former project manager for foresight and transitions, European Environment Agency.
18. Eva Kaili, Member of the European Parliament, Chair of the Panel for the Future of Science and Technology (STOA), European Parliament.
19. Dr. Theo Karapiperis, Head of Unit, Scientific Foresight Unit (STOA), European Parliamentary Research Services, European Parliament.
20. Dr. Johannes Klumpers, Head of Unit, Scientific Advice Mechanism, European Commission.
21. Dr. Christian Kurrer, Policy Analyst, Scientific Foresight Unit (STOA), European Parliamentary Research Service, European Parliament.
22. Charlotte Medland, Impact and Evaluation Officer, Humanities Division, University of Oxford, UK.
23. Dr. Riel Miller, Head of Futures Literacy at UNESCO, Paris, France.
24. Joséphine Rebecca (Fientje) Moerman, judge at the Constitutional Court of Belgium; formerly Minister responsible for Science Policy, Belgium.
25. Dr. Jan Marco Muller, Head of Directorate Office, Coordinator for Science to Policy and Science Diplomacy at International Institute for Applied Systems Analysis (IIASA), Laxenburg, Austria.
26. Dr. Nissy Nevil, Freelance Science Writer, India.

27. Dr. Eamonn Noonan, Policy Analyst, Global Trends Unit, European Parliamentary Research Service, European Parliament.
28. Lesley Paterson, Head, Public Engagement with Research, University of Oxford, UK.
29. Kris Peeters, Mobility expert, Lecturer in Mobility Sciences, Flanders, Belgium.
30. Dr. Jerome R. Ravetz, Associate Fellow, Institute for Science, Innovation and Society at the University of Oxford, UK.
31. Riccardo Ribera d'Alcala, Director-General for Internal Policies of the Union, European Parliament.
32. Dr. Margarida Rodrigues, Co-Chair of Cambridge Science and Policy Forum; Postdoctoral Research Associate, Department of Chemistry, University of Cambridge, UK.
33. Dr. Paul Rübig, Member of the European Parliament, First Vice-Chair of the Panel for the Future of Science and Technology (STOA), European Parliament.
34. Dr. Maurizio Salvi, Senior Policy Analyst, Scientific Advice Mechanism; former Head of the Secretariat of the European Group of Ethics, European Commission.
35. Dr. Raf Scheers, Editor-in-Chief, EOS Magazine, Antwerp, Belgium.
36. Dr. Keith Sequeira, Senior Advisor to the Cabinet of Carlos Moedas, European Commissioner for Research, Science and Innovation, European Commission.
37. Prof. Sir David Spiegelhalter, Professor of Public Understanding of Risk; Executive Director, Winston Centre for Risk and Evidence Communication, University of Cambridge; President of the Royal Statistical Society, UK.
38. Dr. Karen Stroobants, Policy Adviser to the Royal Society of Chemistry, London, UK.
39. Dr. Vladimir Sucha, Director-General, Joint Research Centre, European Commission.
40. Prof. William Sutherland, Miriam Rothschild Professor of Conservation Biology, University of Cambridge, UK.
41. Dr. Jaana Tapanainen, Advisor to the Prime Minister's Office of the United Arab Emirates, Expert in Strategic Foresight; Member of the Finnish Government Foresight Group, Finland.
42. Anthony Teasdale, Director-General, European Parliamentary Research Services, European Parliament.

43. Dr. Chris Tyler, Director Public Policy, Department of Science, Technology, Engineering and Public Policy (STEaPP), University College, London, UK.
44. Dr. Sybille van den Hove, Executive Director, Bridging for Sustainability, Belgium.
45. Kristel Van der Elst, CEO of The Global Foresight Group; Executive Head, Policy Horizons Canada, Government of Canada; Visiting Professor at the College of Europe.
46. Pieter Vandooren, Science Journalist, De Standaard, Groot-Bijgaarden, Belgium.
47. Dr. Sofie Vanthournout, Director Sense about Science EU, Brussels, Belgium.
48. Dr. Koen Vermeir, Member the Global Young Academy and Associate Research Professor at the French National Centre for Scientific Research (CNRS), Paris, France.
49. Arūnas Vinčiūnas, Head of Cabinet of Commissioner Andriukaitis, responsible for Health and Food Safety, European Commission.
50. Tracey Wait, Manager of Foresight, Policy Horizons Canada, Canada.
51. Koen Wauters, Science Journalist, VRT Television, Brussels, Belgium.

APPENDIX B: ADDITIONAL READINGS

Bell, Wendell. 2003. *Foundations of Futures Studies: Volume 1, History, Purposes, and Knowledge: Human Science for a New Era*. Routledge, Taylor & Francis.

Bell, Wendell. 2004. *Foundations of Futures Studies: Volume 2: Values, Objectivity, and the Good Society*. Routledge, Taylor & Francis.

Bishop, Peter C., and Andy Hines. 2012. *Teaching About the Future*. New York: Palgrave Macmillan.

Centre for Strategic Futures, Prime Minister's Office, Singapore. 2017. *Foresight: A Glossary*. www.csf.sg.

Government Office for Science (UK). 2011. *Code of Practice for Scientific Advisory Committees*.https://assets.publishing.service.gov.uk/government/uploads/system/uploads/attachment_data/file/278498/11-1382-code-of-practice-scientific-advisory-committees.pdf.

Lentsch, Justus, and Peter Weingart. 2011. *The Politics of Scientific Advice: Institutional Design for Quality Assurance*. Cambridge: Cambridge University Press.

Meadows, Donella H., and Diana Wright. 2008. *Thinking in Systems: A Primer*. White River Junction, VT: Chelsea Green Publishing.

Organisation for Economic Co-operation and Development. "Scientific Advice for Policy Making: The Role and Responsibility of Expert Bodies and Individual Scientists." IDEAS Working Paper Series from RePEc.

Oreskes, Naomi, and Erik M. Conway. 2010. *Merchants of Doubt: How a Handful of Scientists Obscured the Truth on Issues from Tobacco Smoke to Global Warming*. New York: Bloomsbury Press.

Merchants of Doubt. 2014. Film Directed by Robert Kenner. Sony Pictures Home Entertainment. http://sonyclassics.com/merchantsofdoubt/. Sony Pictures Home Entertainment. 2015. OCLC 913221745.

© The Editor(s) (if applicable) and The Author(s), under exclusive license to Springer Nature Switzerland AG, 2020
L. Van Woensel, *A Bias Radar for Responsible Policy-Making*,
St Antony's Series, https://doi.org/10.1007/978-3-030-32126-0

Pielke, Roger A. 2007. *The Honest Broker: Making Sense of Science in Policy and Politics*. Cambridge: Cambridge University Press.

Schwartz, Peter. 1998 *The Art of the Long View: Planning for the Future in an Uncertain World*. New York: Wiley.

Shell. 2008. *Scenarios: An Explorer's Guide*.https://www.shell.com.

Van der Heijden, Kees. 2005. *Scenarios: The Art of Strategic Conversation*. 2nd ed. Chichester: Wiley.

Van Woensel, Lieve, and Vicky Joseph. 2017. *Forward-Looking Policy-Making at the European Parliament Through Scientific Foresight*. Brussels: European Parliament, PE 603.205. http://www.europarl.europa.eu.

Wilkinson, Angela. 2017. *Strategic Foresight Primer*. Luxembourg: Luxembourg: Publications Office.

Wilsdon, James, and Robert Doubleday. 2015. *Future Directions for Scientific Advice in Europe*. Cambridge: Centre for Science and Policy.

Index

A

Advisory services, 88, 104, 105
Anchoring bias, 26. *See also* Availability
    biases
Associative biases, 21, 23, 26
    bio bias, 26–27. *See also* EU biofuel
        policy (case)
    ethicality bias (good or evil), 26
    nature bias, 26. *See also* Vaccination
    romantic bias, 26, 27
Attention biases, 21, 24, 109
    bias blind spot, 24
    target bias, 26
    tunnel vision, 24, 26
Authority bias, 26, 29, 30. *See also*
    Séralini affair (case study); The
    Lancet; Wakefield-MMR vaccine
    case
Availability biases, 21, 22, 25
    anchoring bias, 26
    authority bias, 26
    knowledge bias, 26
    media bias, 93

B

Backcasting, 42, 43, 60, 61, 64, 65,
    81, 86, 96, 97, 102, 103. *See also*
    Civil Law Rules on Robotics
Bias awareness, 18
Bias blind spot, 24. *See also* Bias
    awareness
Biases, 17, 21
    advisory processes, 18
    associative biases, 26
    attention biases, 24
    availability biases, 25
    bias wheel (tool for bias awareness),
        xiv, 33, 110
    brain and biases, 19
    cognitive biases, 15, 17, 70
    cultural and value biases, 23
    definition, 34
    in evidence, 9
    interest biases, 25
    living with, 20
    origin of the term, 18
    overcoming, 19, 20
    research biases, 21

Bias wheel (tool for bias awareness), 18, 21, 34
Bio bias, 33. *See also* EU biofuel policy (case)
Black swans, 43. *See also* Foresight
Blind spot bias, 24
Blockchain. *See* Trends analysis
Brainstorming
    explorative scenarios, 95
    foresight, 64
    foresight conversations, 57
    societal concerns, 95
    soft impacts, 94

C
Captivology
    disruption triggers, 99
    Parr, B., 97, 104
    reputation trigger, 104. *See also* Authority bias
    stages of attention, 97
Carrots, sticks and sermons, 80, 83
Case of robotics, 64
Chief Scientific Adviser (CSA), 4, 15
    Glover, Anne, 4
    Gluckman, Peter, 7
Civil Law Rules on Robotics, 62
    legislation, 62
Club of Rome, 95. *See also* Meadows, D.
Cognitive biases. *See* Biases
Cognitive dissonance, 18, 20, 28
Communication, 98
    formats, 98
    framing, 99
    framing of evidence, 98
    and maintaining trust, 7
    measles, 99
    policy-makers, 98
    of uncertainty, 91, 100
    virtual Reality, 98

waste management, 99
Compernolle, T., 19, 97
Confirmation bias, 23, 24, 29, 31. *See also* Séralini affair (case study); Wakefield-MMR vaccine case
Conflict of interest bias, 25. *See also* Wakefield-MMR vaccine case
    advocacy, 92
Controversy, 100
Cross-impact analysis, 42
Cross-policy impact assessment, 76, 97. *See also* Doughnut scheme for cross-policy impact assessment
    aims of, xv
    European Parliament's competences, 76
    policy conflicts, 83
    reiteration using doughnut scheme, 78
Cultural and value biases, 21
    confirmation bias, 23
    ideological bias, 23
    in-group bias, 23
    stereotype bias, 21
Cultured meat
    illustration, 61

D
Deer, Brian, 29. *See also* Wakefield-MMR vaccine case
Delphi, 41
Demographic perspective., 55. *See also* STEEPED schema
Doughnut scheme for cross-policy impact assessment, xv, 78, 79, 116
    assessing policy options, 78
    assessment of the impact of policy options, 105
    cross-policy impact analysis, 101
Driving forces, 43. *See also* Foresight

E

Economic perspective, 53. *See also* STEEPED schema

Ecosystem, 11, 14. *See also* Science-policy ecosystem

Emerging issues, 43. *See also* Foresight

preparedness, 109

respond to, 86

Environmental perspective, 54. *See also* STEEPED schema

Environmental Sciences Europe, 28

Envisioning, 42, 44, 59, 63. *See also* Foresight; Visioning

Ethicality bias, 27. *See also* Associative biases

Good or evil, 26

Ethical perspective, 62. *See also* STEEPED schema

EU biofuel policy (case), 24, 31, 32

European Commission, 4

appointment of CSA, 4

European Science Advisors Forum (ESAF), 6

European Food Safety Authority's (EFSA), 61

European Parliament, 76

competences, 76, 77, 83

European Parliamentary Research Service (EPRS), 5

Panel for the Future of Science and Technology (STOA), 10, 41, 95

Scientific foresight process, 62. *See also* Foresight

Evidence, 88

assumptions, 90

knowledge centres, 106

limits of science, 86

perceptions of scientific evidence, 100

selective, 25

synthesis, 9, 88

types of input, 8, 88

unbiased synthesis, 8

Evidence-based policy-making, 9

Experimenter biases, 22. *See also* Wakefield-MMR vaccine case

F

Feedback loops, 103. *See also* Systems analysis

Festinger, L., 20. *See also* Cognitive dissonance

Forecasts, 42, 43

Foresight, 39

aims, 44, 45

and technology assessment, 44, 46

anticipating future events, 62

assistive technologies for people with disabilities, 95

assumptions, 63

backcasting, 44, 60

black swans, 43

brainstorming sessions, 57

collective intelligence, 62

conversations, 40, 49

cross-impact analysis, 42

definition, 39, 40, 57

Delphi (method), 41

desirability, 48

driving forces, 43

emerging issues, 43

envisioning, 42

foresight conversations, 50

future impacts, xiii

group thinking, 41

hard & soft impacts, 46

horizon scanning, 41

in advisory processes, 40

methodologies, 40

normative dimension, 46

participative methodology, 45

phases, 86

possible impacts, 40. *See also* Impacts

purpose, 40
scenario-based foresight, 49
scenarios, 42
terminology, 40
trends analysis, 43
unintended and perverse impacts, 46
visioning, 42. *See also* Envisioning
What if ... questions, 94. *See also*
    Brainstorming
wicked problems, 43
wildcards, 43
wind-tunnelling, 44
Foresight conversations, 60. *See also*
    Brainstorming
interactionist thinking, 58, 65. *See
    also* Thinking, *The Enigma of
    Reason*
Funtowicz, S., 91

G
Genetically modified food, 100
Georghiou, L., 45
Good or evil, 26. *See also* Ethicality bias
Guardians, 96
    bias check, 101
    framework, 101
    integrity of the scientific advisory
        process, 117
    quality assurance, 104. *See also*
        Responsible Scientific Advice
        (RSA)

H
Hard impacts, 46. *See also* Impacts
Honest broker, 8, 89. *See also* Pielke, R.
    earning trust, 100
    role, 10, 11
Horizon scanning, 41

I
Ideological bias, 23

Impacts, 63, 71, 116
    avoidable, 83
    hard, 46, 116
    perverse impacts., 80. *See also*
        Unintended impacts
    possible future, xiv
    soft, 47, 116
    undesirable, 83
    unintended, xv, 34, 46, 71, 76, 80,
        94
Impartiality, 65, 86
    of evidence, 89
    of policy options, 65
    of scientific advisor, 116
Incentivise consumers to purchase
    electric cars (illustrative case),
    74. *See also* Cross-policy impact
    assessment
Influence, 92, 101, 109
    polarization, 108
    social cascades, 109
    social media, 109
Information cascades, 86, 109. *See also*
    Sunstein, C.R.
Interdisciplinarity, 57, 58
Interest-based biases, 25. *See* Interest
    biases
Interest biases, 21
    conflict of interest bias, 25
    self-serving bias, 25
    tactical bias, 25
Interest groups, 13, 14, 25, 70, 71, 91,
    92, 101, 102. *See also* Stakeholders

K
Kahneman, D., 19, 27, 97. *See also*
    Thinking, thinking fast and slow
Kello, L., 58, 59
Knowledge bias, 26, 108. *See also* Avail-
    ability biases; Wakefield-MMR
    vaccine case
Knowledge centres, 106

European Environment Agency (EEA), 89
European Food Safety Authority (EFSA), 89
European Space Agency (ESA), 89
Food and Agriculture Organization (FAO), 31
Intergovernmental Panel on Climate Change (IPCC), 89
International Energy Agency (IEA), 89
Joint Research Centre, EC (JRC), 89
Oxford Martin School, 89
Research agencies, 89
Scientific advisory bodies, 4, 6
Think tanks, 89
US's National Aeronautics and Space Administration (NASA), 89

L
Limits of science, 86. *See also* Trust
Lobbyists, 25
Luhmann, N., 13

M
McGann, J.G., 89. *See also* Think tanks
Meadows, D., 13, 70
Measles, 30. *See also* Vaccination; Wakefield-MMR vaccine case
Media, 7, 13, 28, 93, 97, 105, 106, 110
Media bias, 26
Merchants of doubt, 15, 25. *See also* Oreskes, N. and Conway, E.M.
Mercier, H., 58. *See also* Thinking, *The Enigma of Reason*

N
Nature bias, 26, 27. *See also* Wakefield-MMR vaccine case

Neutrality, 8
Non-governmental organizations (NGOs), 60, 101, 107, 108. *See also* Stakeholders
David in the fight with Goliath, 107

O
Objectivity of science, 90. *See also* Impartiality
Oreskes, N. and Conway, E.M., 14, 25, 26, 92

P
Parliamentary advisory bodies, 4
Pielke, R., 8, 10, 14, 20, 89. *See also* Honest broker
Policy alternatives, 10. *See also* Policy options
Policy-making, 9, 48, 62
    cross-policy impact assessment, 78
    democracy, 9
    emergency, 109
    evidence-based, xiii, 9
    hard and soft impacts, 46
    perverse impacts, 46
    policy problems, 91
    technocratic, 9
    unintended impacts, 46
Policy options, 10, 64, 71, 78, 96
    adaptation, 81
    assessment, 12
    'carrots', 80
    cross-policy impact assessment, 74
    desirability, 48, 64, 83, 96
    development and assessment, 96
    evidence-based, 10
    future-proof, 110
    innovative solutions, 81
    limitations, 81
    mitigation, 80
    multiple perspectives, 57

ratio of benefit to harm, 55
reform, 81
selection, 80
'sermons', 80
'sticks', 80
Post-Normal Science (PNS), 91. *See
also* Funtowicz, S.; Ravetz, J.
Precautionary Principle, 94. *See also*
Responsible Scientific Advice
(RSA)
Precision agriculture
case, 60
Public opinion, 14, 15, 85, 92, 109.
See also Societal perspective
social media impact, 101

Q
Quality assurance, 105
sources of evidence, 105

R
Ravetz, J., 90, 91, 94
Reporting bias, 22, 26. *See also* Séralini
affair
Research biases, 21, 22
experimenter bias, 22
reporting bias, 22
sampling bias, 21
sponsorship bias, 23
Research questions, 86
framing, 86
Responsible Research and Innovation
(RRI), 59
Responsible Scientific Advice (RSA)
anticipatory, 116
brainstorming, 93
criteria, 3
evidence-based, 115
framework, 111
holistic, 116
inclusive, 116

non-governmental organizations
(NGOs), 108
reflective, 116
responsive, 116
scientific advice, 101
scientific evidence, 108
Who guards the guardians?, 91. *See
also* Guardians
Romantic bias, 26, 27
Round up herbicide (case study), 27,
28. *See also* Séralini affair (case
study)

S
Sampling biases, 21
Scenario-based foresight, 40, 47, 48,
70, 87
explorative scenarios, 95
Scenarios. *See also* 42. *See also* Foresight
definition, 48
driving forces, 43
explorative, 48–50, 65, 103
futures, 96
Science policy, 7
Science-policy ecosystem, xv, 11, 14,
15, 71, 85, 87, 93
actors, 93
advisory process, 85
food waste, 11
holistic view, 87
scientific advisory process, 14
zooming out, 110
Science-policy interfaces, 10
Centre for Science and Policy
(CSaP), 6
Scientific advice, 2
communicating, xv, 97
institutional structures, 3, 4
need, 2
political and legal perspectives, 54.
See also STEEPED schema

Scientific advisers, 96. *See also*
    Guardians
  evidence-based, 10
  networks, 6
  responsibility, 117
  roles, 1, 10
Scientific advising, 1
  legislative, 86
  practices, 7
  research questions, 86
  scoping, 87
Scientific advisory bodies, 4
  Danish Board of Technology (DBT),
    5
  European Parliamentary Technology
    Assessment (EPTA), 7
  Finland's committee for the future, 5
  governmental, 4
  Institute of Technology Assessment
    (ITA), 5
  International Network for Govern-
    ment Science Advice (INGSA),
    6
  Netherland's Scientific Council for
    Government Policy (WRR), 6
  Norwegian Board of Technology
    (NTB), 5
  Office of Technology Assessment
    (TAB), 5
  Panel for the Future of Science and
    Technology (STOA), 5
  Parliamentary Office for Evaluation
    of Scientific and Technological
    Options (OPECST), 5
  Parliamentary Office of Science and
    Technology (POST), 5
  Rathenau Institute, 5
  Scientific Advice Mechanism (SAM),
    4
  UK's Parliamentary Office of Science
    and Technology (POST), 7
Scientific advisory process, 11

  and foresight phase, 44
  identification and framing phases, 86
  practical toolkit, 116
  research question, 86
  responsible scientific advice (RSA),
    85. *See also* Responsible
    Research and Innovation (RRI)
  scoping, 102, 103. *See also* Policy
    options
  systems analysis, 69
Scientific advisory services, 86, 104,
    105. *See also* Scientific advisory
    bodies
Scientific evidence, 6, 7. *See* Evidence
  contextualizing, 110
Scientific foresight, xiv
Sea level rise (considering alternative
    policy options illustration), 80
  assessment, 83. *See also* Cross-policy
    impact assessment
Self-driving cars, 61, 62
  backcasting, 61
Self-serving bias, 25
Senge, P.M., 13, 70
Séralini affair (case study), 27
Sermons, 80
Shell Oil Company, 'scenarios', 48
Societal Perspective, 52. *See also*
    STEEPED schema
  concerns, 95
  desirability, 64
  opportunities and concerns, 63
  stakeholders views, 88
Soft impacts, 47. *See also* Hard impacts;
    Policy-making, unintended
    impacts
Sperber, D., 58. *See also* Thinking, *The
    Enigma of Reason*
Sponsorship bias, 22, 25
Stakeholders, 8, 11, 12, 15, 48, 57, 59,
    60
  advocacy groups, 92, 96

analysis, 60, 63, 115
civil-society organizations, 92
engagement with stakeholders, 87
experts, 96
industry, 89
interest groups, 92
lobbying groups, 92. *See also*
    Lobbyists
media, 92
model, 10
policy-makers, 104
preferences, 48, 90
pressure groups, 92
societal stakeholders, 59
STEEPED schema, 63, 71, 77, 80, 81,
    88, 94, 105, 110
analysis, 57
brainstorming, 57
demographic perspective, 55
economic perspective, 53
electric cars illustration, 80
environmental perspective, 54
envisioning, 57. *See also* STEEPED
    schema
ethical perspective, 55
for stakeholder analysis, 63
in advisory process, 101
in foresight process, 57
political and legal, 54
process, 57
societal perspective, 52
technological perspective, 52
Stereotype bias, 23, 24. *See also*
    Cultural and value biases
STOA (European Parliament's Panel
    for the Future of Science and
    Technology), 4
Strategic foresight, 43
Sunstein, C.R., 109
Sustainable Development Goals
    (SDGs), 72–74, 76, 83
electric cars illustration, 74

Swierstra, T., 46, 47. *See also* Soft
    impacts
SWOT analysis, 50. *See also* STEEPED
    schema
Systems analysis, 87, 101. *See also*
    Systems thinking
components, 87
definition, 69
description, 70
feedback loops, 78, 111, 115
holistic view, 87
inward, 70, 71
outward, 71
outward systems analysis, 71, 93
Systems thinking, 13, 43
inward systems thinking, 69–71
outward systems analysis, 69
outward systems thinking, 70
practice, 70
Schaveling and Bryan, 71

T
Tactical bias, 25, 29. *See also* Séralini
    affair (case study)
consequences, 25
Target bias, 24, 32. *See also* EU biofuel
    policy (case)
Technological perspective, 52. *See also*
    STEEPED schema
Technologies
'hard' and 'soft' impacts, 103
unintended and perverse impacts, 46
Technology assessment (TA), 4, 5, 40,
    41
bodies, 4
definition, 44, 45
technical horizon scan, 74. *See also*
    Foresight
Thinking, 57
cross-disciplinarity, 58. *See also*
    Interdisciplinarity

group thinking, 58, 59. *See also*
    Interactive thinking
interactive thinking, 58
interdisciplinarity, 58, 59, 63. *See
    also* Multidisciplinarity
intuitive thinking (thinking fast), 19
multidisciplinarity, 58, 59. *See also*
    Interdisciplinarity
reasoning, 58. *See also* Thinking, *The
    Enigma of Reason*
reflecting brain, 97
reflective thinking (thinking slow),
    19, 26
reflex brain, 19, 97
The Enigma of Reason, 19, 58
thinking fast and slow, 19, 97. *See
    also* Kahneman, D.
Unidisciplinarity, 58
Thinking In Systems: A Primer, 70. *See
    also* Meadows, D.
Think tanks, 5, 88, 89, 106
    quality criteria, 105
Tobacco industry and cancer research,
    92. *See also* Conflict of interest bias
Toolkit for scientific advisers, 116
    bias wheel, 116
    Doughnut scheme for assessing
        cross-policy impacts, 116
    framework of the scientific advisory
        process, 116
    science-policy ecosystem, 116
    STEEPED scheme, 116

Trends analysis, 43. *See also* Foresight
Trust, 34
    impartiality, 86. *See also* Honest
        broker
    maintaining, 7
    mistrust of science, 108
    non-governmental organisations
        (NGOs), 107, 108
    quality assurance, 105
    scientific evidence, 106, 108
    scientists, 108
Tunnel vision, 24, 26, 32. *See also* Blind
    spot bias; EU biofuel policy (case)

V
Vaccination, 30. *See also* Wakefield-
    MMR vaccine case
    nature bias, 31. *See also* Vaccination;
        Wakefield-MMR vaccine case
Value biases, 23. *See also* Cultural and
    value biases
Van Woensel, Peter, 82. *See also* Sea
    level rise (considering alternative
    policy options illustration)
Visioning, 42

W
Wakefield-MMR vaccine case, 21, 29
Wicked problems, 43
Wilkinson, A., 40, 48, 57
Wind-tunnelling, 44. *See also* Scenarios

Printed by Printforce, the Netherlands